T0208259

# By GRACE AND GRACE Alone

Shiloyne

authorHOUSE®

*AuthorHouse*™
*1663 Liberty Drive*
*Bloomington, IN 47403*
*www.authorhouse.com*
*Phone: 833-262-8899*

*Published by AuthorHouse  03/20/2023*

*ISBN: 979-8-8230-0229-5 (sc)*
*ISBN: 979-8-8230-0227-1 (hc)*
*ISBN: 979-8-8230-0228-8 (e)*

*Library of Congress Control Number: 2023903762*

# CONTENTS

# PROLOGUE

Life is not always happening as planned. Whether we put one foot in front of the other or one pants leg on at a time, we have no guarantee to constant happiness, pain, love, freedom, or comfort in this existence that we call life. But who wants pain. Yet, pain teaches us valuable lessons.

We are born with two parents. Whether they love us in the long term of our lives is sometimes questionable, yet they do their best in most cases.

The forty-three years of my life on this planet exposed me to a great deal of life that shaped my existence into a humble, yet ambitious human being. My childhood was fun as well as rocky at times, but those whom have come and gone left valuable knowledge through loving, harsh, remorseful, compassionate interaction over the years. In writing this book, I only intend to show gratitude as well as understanding of events that my readers may or may not have in common; not in an attempt to achieve fame or ridicule. However, JUDGEMENT is unavoidable.

I love everything and everyone that was created with the understanding that feelings are not going to always be mutual. Let's face it, Good and Evil are not always understood, however, we live in a world where we have consequences for our actions….. most of the time. Those consequences are not always desirable and when they are desirable, they are not always long lasting.

If my reader learns anything in reading this book, I hope they learn to live in peace and offer peace to those whom come across their path because they never truly know the past.

**I**

$\sim\!\!\mathcal{o}\mathcal{o}\mathcal{o}\!\!\sim$

$\mathcal{T}$he things that shape us are said to be known and intended by Creator….God.

1978 was just as good as any other year to be born. For some of us, it was the year of the copyright. For me, it was a Tuesday in April at a clinic operated by Dr. Lungsford. My Mother, Rosie, was giving birth at 1:09 a.m. to "Shiloyne".

She said I was born with a 109 degree temperature so I had to be placed in a tub of ice. I guess the will of life was strong in me.

I had the average childhood as I remember. It was me and my mother and a man named Charles whom I knew as my father. He came into my life in about 1983, when my brother Jeremy was born. The memory of my grandfather Frank, Charles's father, comes into mind to begin by going to help my grandfather on his farm with the cows and the fences as well as witness an eye surgery he had to have for glaucoma and caterdfs.

I was roughly 8 years old and my grandmother Rosie Bee was

still alive. My Grandfather Frank was a janitor, bus driver, deacon, farmer, and Mason. So discipline was a must. My Grandmother Rosie Bee was a single, 59 year old woman with a huge family. My Grandfather Matthew had long since moved on. Me, mom, and my brother Jeremy were living in Como, MS with my grandmother Rosie on 310.

My Mother picked me up from Como Elementary and allowed me to drive home across the Santa Fe railroad track to where we lived with 4 of her 9 sisters and my grandmother. Back in 1985, not many people were on the road at that time of the day in a small town such a Como. Its said to be the richest town on the map in Mississippi.

We made it to the house safely. She had been allowing or teaching me to drive since I was 5 years old and my fascination of cars due to her racing her Chevy Nova in her spare time on her days off from a Furniture Company. She would win 50 dollars a pop here and there, which would help out on my school clothing and diapers for my brother. But he was coming out of the "Luvs" and "Huggies" into regular cloths. Besides he was about 3 yrs old.

I got out the car, DUKES OF HAZAARD style and threw my mom the keys. Then ran around and picked my baby brother up to go into the house. We were all packed already to go to Charles house for the weekend.

We made it to Charles's house and Granddaddy Frank was already happy to see up. He knew I was going to help him in the reading area since he had stopped school at a young age to take care of his family and Grandma Zela whom hand passed away in 1973. He was a Deacon at Mt. Peel Missionary Baptist Church in Holly Springs. However, his surgery had made it hard for him to see. I was in fourth grade in 1985, but I could read and write very well. I was on the Dean's List, the Principal Scroll, the Honor Roll and I took advanced classes. At night I went to Galena School and assisted Granddaddy Frank with his night studies to get his GED. He was born in 1920, but he had only a 3$^{rd}$ grade education. All that he could do was print his name.

We got out the car and I grabbed our bags and took them into Granddaddy Frank's house. Mom went straight to Granddaddy Frank and kissed him on the cheek and he said Charles was somewhere cutting grass like normal. That's what he did for work. He cut yards as well as side construction. Well it was 1985; not much money was really needed to survive and look appropriate.

Mom began to prepare the favorite breakfast.

Fried chicken, white rice, and homemade biscuits cooked done, but not completely done with a golden brown top. Charles came in from cutting grass with his usual water bottle canteen, filled with corn whiskey; ready to eat.

We gathered around the table and began to say grace. I led in prayer.

"Dear God,
   Thank YOU for watching over me and giving me
   the strength to make it this far throughout my days,
   Watch over my friends family and loved ones.
   Keep them safe in your arms forever. AMEN"

Charles had already started eating because he was KING OF THE CASTLE as he called himself. All of a sudden he coughed. Since I was sitting across from him; rice expelled from his mouth, came across the table and landed in my rice. As if it were some father to son transfer in the worst way. At the time, I had no praise or amusement to give and no one notice but me. My grandfather yelled for Charles to cover his mouth…. In the middle of prayer. I, on the other hand, was not touching my rice.

I finished the prayer, and ate around the rice. After Breakfast, Me and Granddaddy went back out to the pasture to feed the cows and count them to make sure there weren't any missing. Granddaddy Frank also had pride in his livestock and his land. Along the walk we would check the fences to see if any space were wide enough so the cows could get out. On occasion, a bull or a heifer would get out by jumping or breaking through old wire. We would repair the fence after the feeding of the cows. He still had patches over his eyes from the surgery he had just gone through so he need me to help him nail in the u-bolt nails. He would chop down a tree, dig a hole with the post-hole digger, and fill-in the space along the fence so the cow could not get out again. He had about 25 cows on 3 acres of land. And we share land surrounding that with neighboring farmers. Life was good, but it was hard work. Especially for an 8 yr old. We finished the task at hand that was on my grandfather's land and had no cows to go looking for nor had anyone called to let my grandfather know of any damage to their fences on their properties. So we went back to the house.

Charles and Reese were house hunting so once they were married, we would not have to stay in my grandfather's house.

Me and my brother shared a room in our grandfather's house. We would jump back and forth from bed to bed doing flips in the air. On one instance, I flipped and did not jump hard enough. In my landing I almost broke my neck as I was unconscious from hitting my head on the side of the cast iron bed frame. For a moment I was unconscious. I didn't mention it to anyone but my brother revived me by slapping my face. Since I was the oldest, I didn't want to get in trouble for being hurt. I never tried it again.

We stayed at my grandfather's house for the rest of the weekend and returned to Como on Sunday night so I could be ready for school the next day at Como Elementary. My mom did the usual. She left my brother with Charles and I went to my cousins while she went to work Sunday evening to get off at the 1:00 a. m. She would then drive to pick me up at around 1:30 in morning from my Great Aunt's house. I loved going to her house to play with my cousins who were much older than me. Well, they were at least 8 years older.

My grandmother's sister was full figured and soft spoken as I remember. She had 3 of my other cousins and an older cousin living with her, as well, as my Uncle Jack. I had been going there as my babysitter for years but I guess I had gotten old enough to be invited to play the new games...... so to speak.

The neighbors and relatives around my Great Aunts house had horses and cows as well. Sometimes during the animal shows they would allow us to sit on the horses and rub the cows.

One day we were playing in the pasture behind Aunt Baby's house and the cows were in the distance. My oldest cousin, Jimmy, was beginning to tease and throw sticks and rocks and make loud noises at the animals for some reason. My female cousin, Tuts, asked him to stop because the animals would get upset. Chris remained quiet. Nevertheless, Jimmy continued.

Eventually, one of the bull started behaving as if it was pissed off at us because the herd to begin moving towards us. As they got closer, Tuts and I begin to turn around and move back in the direction of the fence. The animals began to move faster and faster in our direction. The fence was about 200 or 300 feet away from us so we had to run. As we were running the cows were coming from all directions. We had to make it to the fence; climb it or crawl under and get to the other side. Jimmy, Chris and Tuts passed me and had already made it over and through the fence.

They were all screaming for me to run faster because the cows were catching up to me. I didn't have enough time to climb the fence so I slid under the fence as if I was sliding to first base. They helped me up off the ground and asked if I was okay. I said, "Yes".

We got in the house and Aunt Baby had cooked her "family famous" chicken dumpling with yellow cornbread. I loved the way she cooked it. We could actually smell it from outside and when we got inside the house, the aroma filled the air. It was mouth-watering.

Tuts went to her room to do some homework and play with her dolls while Jimmy and Chris went to the room they were sharing to play Nintendo. I was sitting in the front room waiting to get a sample of the dumpling.

## 2

was about 10 years younger than my older cousins. However, life was already unfolding. My mom was working at a Furniture in Senatobia, MS. She would allow me to go to my Aunt Baby's house since I was tall for my age and need big kids to play with. Besides, I loved going over there because we'd play all sorts of games and I could have a little fun after school.

My mom worked the evening shift that would let her get off work at about one o'clock in the morning. She would then make it to Great Aunt Baby's house to pick me up in the darkness of morning and take us home to Grandma's house.

One day Tuts wanted to play a new game since I was getting older. The game was called "House". It's a game that allows us to behave or mimic the behavior that goes on in the household such as father, son, mother, daughter, brother, sister, relative, etc. In the beginning it was just she and I playing the game in her room. Then, she called Jimmy in to play the father role. It was a very innocent game. However, it could get out of hand or cause questionable behavior. Since I was being babysat, Tuts pretended that I was her child and Jimmy pretended to be the Father. She was to pretend to be Jimmy's girlfriend/ wife.

Eventually the game ended. On some occasions I would be the father and Jimmy would be the child or Chris would become the father and Tuts would always be the mother or my sister because we we're literally behaving like adults that we saw throughout the family or within the community. We played that game for majority of the summer and most of the fall as far as I remember but nothing never became "questionable"… at first.

I was at my home with my Grandmother. It was holiday season and family was in and out of the house. Amongst me, my brother, and my mother there was two of my mothers' sisters as well as there children living in the house under my Grandmother's roof. I was the oldest grandchild so I felt some sense of responsibility in looking over my cousins.

Grandmother had cooked a big dinner for the men that would come over from within the community. There was an older man well over 40 named Mr. Golding that would come over. He was a member of the Church.

Everyone had left the dinner gathering and it was just Grandma, Mr. Golding and me in the house. It was in the winter time. Grandma was doing something in the kitchen and I was in the back with Mr. Golding. She called out to Mr. Golding to tell him to keep an eye on me while she washed the dishes.

We live in what's called a "shotgun house. It was a nice sized house but it was an open house. When you walked in the front door there was a wall that separated the two sides. The kitchen was in the back of the house.

Mr. Golding asked me to come over and sit on his leg. So I did so. As I sat there here began to ask me all kinds of questions. Then the "questionable" behavior happened. While my grandmother was in the kitchen, Mr. Golding whipped out his penis and grabbed my hand and placed it on his penis. My grandmother called my name.

"Shaun", she said.

"Ma'am", I responded.

She said, "Bring Mr. Golding's plates to the kitchen when he is done so I can wash them".

Immediately, Mr. Golding's, placed one finger to his lips and said, "This will be between us boys". Handed me his plate and zipped his pants. I took the plates to my grandmother and she washed them.

I didn't say anything to my Grandmother about what Mr. Golding did because I honestly did not understand what took place. When I went back to the room Mr. Golding had moved to a different seat so he could get a better angle of Grandma and make his move on me. Since he knew Grandma was going to be a while he didn't force me to perform oral sex on his penis. After he was done with a few minutes he zipped up again; stood up and informed my grandmother that he was going to be leaving.

I was upset and remember being upset because it was a painful, uncomfortable situation.

I didn't even tell my mother because of the age of Mr. Golding and the reputation he had within our household as well as the community. I was simply too young to understand that my innocence had just been stripped.

I waited like a angry warrior for the next time I would see Mr. Golding because I was going to defend myself as a 8 yr older. So I motivated my cousins to attack Mr. Golding the next time he came over.

Mr. Golding came over to the house to visit my grandmother. Unknowingly, I had informed my younger cousins of his actions so I prepared them. We sat on the steps of the porch waiting for him to get to the edge of the steps. We had forks and butterknives. We leaped off the porch and attacked Mr. Golding stabbing him with those forks and butterknives as best as we could in my defense. Mr. Golding's amazement at my behavior made him quickly retreat to his car making up some excuse for not being able to come into the house. We were not strong enough to do any serious damage to him, but we did cause pain. He never came back to visit and he passed away due to natural cause as far a I remember.

When I went back to Aunt Baby's house Tuts was teasing me about attacking Mr. Golding and I told her why I got our little cousins to help me do so. She explained that I did the right thing but was still damaged.

I guess to somehow correct the damage to my innocence as a child she chose to inform me about things that had happened to her. My life unfolded more.

The game of "house" was evolving. We were passed "questionable" behavior. Yet it was still innocent.

After playing "house" for a few months I ended up being over my cousin's mother's house to spend the night with Jimmy and Chris in Sardis, MS. I was asleep when I felt I was being hit by something. Jimmy and Chris were throwing shoes at me in order to tease me for playing house the night before with a girl who spent the night at Pat's house with us as well. The night before, I was playing in the girl's vagina with my fingers because she asked me to. That's just how far things had come due to the game of "house". The girl woke up and told them that I had done so. So they decided to tease me for my adult like behavior by waking me up out of my sleep with the pain of shoes

10

being thrown at me. After a few painful throws, I jumped out of the bed with no questions asked and charged at them like an angry bull. The ran into the bathroom where cousin Pat, Tuts' mom, was taking a bath. I kicked the door off the hinges, literally. Pat jumped out of her bathwater, naked, and yelled at me to stop. So I did. I informed her why I was doing so. She understood, but still upset.

**3**

The Thanksgiving holiday had just passed in 1985. I was doing exceptional in school and was allowed to take advance classes. I had been promoted to 5<sup>th</sup> grade at Como Elementary. However, my mother was still holding off on marrying Charles and I was still going to Granddaddy Frank's house to help out on the farm. I was really strong for my age as well as smart. I attended night classes with Granddaddy Frank on Tuesday and Thursday to help him with his Math and English so he could finish his education. His eye was still healing from surgery. He asked me to put his eye drops in his eyes on time and help him to be reminded. Things were going pretty well on the outside looking in, but from the inside looking out….. they were beginning to unfold even more.

Grandma had a major dislike of Charles, my known to be father. She didn't approve of him wanting to marry my mother. However, since my brother was coming on 3 yrs old, my parents wanted their own house… at least.

At that age I understood as much as I could about human behavior.

I didn't understand much about people but I knew about GOD. Going to church with my grandparents on both sides of my family was a regular thing to do. I was just learning right and wrong, good and evil, fair and unfair, finding reason. Looking for causes and affects/effects of my existence. I had already been molested and I was having very painful stomach aches due to stress from what had happened to me. Not knowing the damage of the molestation in its fullest. I no longer wanted to shake hands or be touchy feely. I didn't have any reason to question sexuality but I questioned human affection from that moment on. Mainly, because I was forced in to knowledge or the ways of MAN. Whether I wanted to know or not...... I knew.

It was Christmas Eve. Every one was over for dinner.

Lots of loud talking and laughter going on throughout the house and grandma. Nasa was getting ready to launch the Challenger Space Shuttle in the following month. I was simply waiting to open the rest of my Christmas presents. I had a Star Wars set. All the characters. I wanted to become and Astronaut when I grew up because I felt like I would be closer to GOD or more "One with the Universe"... so to speak. I love discussing all the creations of GOD that I could understand.

My mother was still at work so once again I was somewhat unguarded. There was a lot of activity going on in the house. We had no running water so we had to fill buckets and jugs with water from our neighbor in order to keep hygiene and cleanliness.

In the bathroom, there was no light and no toilet. My oldest cousin was in the bathroom and asked me to pass him some toilet paper. I had to go ask one of the adults for the toilet paper. I guess the past months of playing the game "house" had mad him want to take things further. So…. As I passed him the toilet paper, he grabbed my wrist and pulled me into the dark bathroom. The encounter went much further than what Mr. Golding had forced me to do. It was very painful and unwanted. I thought I had to keep that to myself and amongst us youngsters. He was over 10 yrs. older than me, but we both were still technically, minors.

I guess he had already been molested as well and was simply passing on what he understood as normal. I was no longer a virgin at that moment. Unknowing what was about to unfold, I stopped being happy and raised my guard. I questioned everything from that moment on. My identity as a human was being transformed.

# 4

remember being in the classroom when the 5mc, the school announcement box, sounded off with the school secretary asking for a moment of silence due to the Challenger Space Shuttle exploding. I had just recently transferred from Como Elementary to Galena Elementary School since Charles and Reese were about to enroll my younger brother into kindergarten and they wanted us both to go to the same school. I was still writing my name in the name on my birth certificate but Charles was upset that I wanted to use the last name

I was born with instead of the name he was trying to give me.

The principal of the school, Mrs. Anderson, was a relative, as well as many other teachers at the school. Charles came into the school and spoke with the teachers and insisted that they make me write my last as Moore. There was no legal documentation. He cursed me out in front of the classroom. I was devastated. Completely embarrassed.

After that, my classmates would tease me and talk about me consistently. They would talk about Charles because of the way he looked. They would not hesitate to call me punk and faggot simply because of the relationship I had with Charles in the classroom on that day.

My Mother and Charles got into a huge argument about the writing of my name and on that day I witness my mother get beaten because she was defending the name she had given me. However; since, my younger brother carried Charles' last name on his birth certificate, I felt I was protecting her by writing my name as Charles wanted.

Eventually, Granddaddy Frank retired and Charles took his place as the janitor of Galena Elementary. Now… the events that went on at home were with me at the school but no one in the class knew of the occasional fights.

I started having nose bleeds and severe stomach aches due to stress. Peer pressure came in all forms.

All my progress at one school was erased when I transferred. I was forced to attend the grade in school that correlated to my age instead of my intelligence. I was placed in fifth grade even though I was taking eighth grade courses at Como Elementary. Depression began to be a part of my life when I first opened my mouth to read in the classroom. Everyone would laugh at the way I articulated the words in my pronunciation. I simply wanted to return to Como Elementary, but I eventually got over it.

It was early in the morning in May. Grandma was not up to get me up for school. She was laying on the floor. I walked over and tried to wake her up. She had passed away in her sleep. The family was overwhelmed with grief.

I remember being at the funeral. My mother in her tiny, black and gray, checkerboard dress suit; black high heels. My brother in her arms crying. I was a wreck. It was the first death I had encountered. Devastating.

We had a big dinner after the funeral. I was so stressed of full of separation anxiety. My nose would bleed constantly. We had to leave. The stress of loosing my grandmother felt as though I lost my protector. My mother decided to marry Charles and we moved in over the weekend. Life was on uncharted territory. My mother was just trying to remain focused on the next phase of life. Even she wasn't ready for what was about to unfold. GOD seemed unreal. Well… the love GOD was hard to differentiate from the love of Man.

# 5

Letting go is the hardest thing to do. Being removed from one living situation is supposed to become better. In most cases things do become better.

Living at my grandfather house was a child paradise if you were a country boy like me. I loved getting in my playing clothes and getting dirty; learning the land of my grandfather on Charles's side of the family. He had three brothers and 2 sisters and a two aunts that I was very fund of who live in Kentucky, and St. Louis and Chicago. On the Moore's side of the family we have large family reunions. On the Porter side of the family I was busy knowing all 10 of my mother's sisters and five brothers, so I was always missing or returning to Como to spend the night with my mother's nieces and nephews.

Charles was driving our big grayish green and we had a blow out on one of the back tires. He wanted to teach me how to change a tire and I was eager to learn. We had a pretty good relationship despite his and my mother arguments because at the time their fights were only verbal. The way he spoke was fast, deep talking and sometime muffled to the point I couldn't understand him because he mostly used profanity and I hadn't heard any profanity up to this point.

Needless to say, I was not strong enough to force the lug nut to come off so Charles was getting frustrated.

I was not accustomed to responding in the words "yes sir" or "no sir" so Charles yelled and said, "What did you say to me". And immediately disciplined me with a belt to the behind. It was my first whipping for being what was considered as disobedient. He told my mother that I was talking back to him. I was crying and crying was something my mother hated to see me do.

She raised her voice at Charles and he immediately slapped her. It was the first time I ever seen violence towards my mother. I screamed and cried for Charles to stop and he wouldn't. My mother began to defend herself but Charles continued so I called for granddaddy Frank since there was no 911 in existence at the time. Granddaddy Frank came immediately and he and Charles began to argue. I was glad that he stopped them from fighting.

We didn't stay under the roof of Granddaddy Frank for too much longer. Reese decided to marry Charles and the the mobile home that she had placed in Como was placed in Holly Springs. I transferred school and life went in the direction that it was going.

Granddaddy Frank resigned from being the janitor at Galena and Charles took his place. He wanted me to help him clean up after school as I had done with his father, Granddaddy Frank. His father would pay me after school for working with him to help clean up the school after the evening bus route, but Charles wouldn't pay me because he said the money was going to the house. So working for Charles became a chore. Granddaddy Frank continued going to night school. It was difficult to adjust to being paid for working and not gettin paid for working and being treated as if I was unloved.

Charles had not signed my birth certificate so it was just hearsay and taking my mother's word that he was my biological father, so it was hard to accept the way he treated my mother and be my boss or father.

I participated in any and everything I could that school had to offer just so I could stay busy an possibly not have to help with cleaning up the school anymore. I was too young to get a job and really did not need one other than to show some form of responsibility at a very young age. During the summers I would attend a program called NYSP., the National Youth Sports Program at Rust College and I would work in the fields of local sharecroppers picking peas by the bushel. Once I got my first summer job I started buy-in gym own clothes for school to help my parents out with the stress.

Life was not normal but from the outside looking in a person would think it was. Whether from fear or discipline, we never spoke of what went on in the home. Charles kept a steady job with the school despite his alcohol and drug use. My mom kept her scares and bruises hidden and me and my brother were always on the best behavior we could. Me and my brother were five years apart in age so a lot of times I was trusted to watch the house while my parents were gone to work. Besides, we had our grandfather in front in one house. His sister was next to him. My uncle and his wife were next door. With four houses on the property, there was always someone watching or looking out.

We were playing on our bikes between Granddaddy Frank's and Great Aunt Magnolia's house. We were riding in circles around his old 1986 black Cadillac De'ville. It was my younger cousin Lashaunda, my brother Jeremy and I. Granddaddy Frank was sitting on the porch watching as we continued trying to catch each other on our bikes. He warned us to not ride so close to each other so we don't accidentally run into each other. We eventually began riding in opposite directions and collided with each other. Lashaunda fell off her bike and began crying. Her father, uncle Lucious came to her rescue. He was in the back at his house and heard his daughter's cry out loud when she fell so he came running.

Granddaddy Frank didn't have time to explain to Uncle Lucious that it was an accident so Uncle Lucious immediately grabbed me in the chest. His fingernails caused a deep scratch on my chest which caused me to bleed as he considered himself disciplining me for the accident since I was the oldest. I ran and told my mother and she saw my chest. She immediately called Lashaunda's mother, Aunt Maureen. She explained that it was wrong of Uncle Lucious to scratch me and discipline me for a harmless accident. As good behavior she wanted me to ask Lashaunda was she ok and did I intend to cause her to fall off her bike. Regardless, I was the blame even if they decided it was easier to catch me if they changed directions.

I guess Uncle Lucious felt sorry about scratching me because he apologized. The damage was already done though. The next day the school nurse was giving me penicillin shots for infection. My mother was furious. She said to Aunt Maureen, "I'd poison the hell out of Lucious if he touch him again."

There was a lot to deal with. Whatever plans GOD had, I didn't understand at the moment.

I got more involved with school. Stayed over after for basketball and track practices. Me and my brother began to make friends but were in different age groups when its came to class verse home life. I was often in class with students who where much older than I. Sometimes the older students would tease me for the way my father sounded when he spoke and they would already call me gay and said I looked like an African. They said I sounded white and they would call me out of my name because they knew I had a name change. Some classes where in my age group but most were not.

We were in Mr. Moffit's class sharing textbooks. We were asked to present our homework on the board and sit in groups of fours. I was in a class for Seventh graders when I was supposed to be in Fifth grade. The students would often say I looked like a girl instead of a boy.

I was siting with three other boys and one of the boys began to rub between my legs from under the desk. I did not want to cause a scene so I tried to ignore it and act as if nothing was going on. I mostly tickled but it was still uncomfortable because this time it was in a school setting and my father was right down the hallway. I couldn't take it no more so I raised my hand and snitched to Mr. Moffit. The student got a paddling which only made him upset. It also caused me to receive dislike as the school snitch. I was so uncomfortable to walk into the classroom on most days that it would cause severe stomach aches and nose bleeds with ulcers. I had learn to accept life and what it had to offer. I couldn't continue to suffer from stress due to how people saw me in their eyes. If gay was lifestyle that GOD had in store for me, it was happening fast.

My Grandfather was attending another math class at night at Galena. It was time for him to take a test so I had to walk out of the classroom. Other children were there as well with parents and we were going to have a sleep over at the gym as a form of camping. Children from other schools and of all ages. There was a boy named Rodger who was adopted that was on the playground as I waited for my grandfather to finish testing. He wanted to wrestle me for some sexual advantage and for some reason as boy I loved to wrestle but not for sexual advantages. I guess age make the mind go curious. But I was sure that it would be a fair match.

We began to wrestle. I knew I I was strong from dealing with the cows on the farm, but I had never had to wrestle against another human other than playing at home with my younger brother. Rodger had other plans. I guess he had been exposed to more in life than I had because he wanted to wrestle for sex. I figured it was a friendly competition and I had no interest in sex. I participated. We wrestled like two warriors on the playground that was completely empty in pitch blackness behind the school with the gym in the distance. He was much more aggressive than I thought. Before the match was over he was already having an erection. I guess that was human nature at an early age. We were no more than twelve years old but both had had already been exposed to sexual behavior. There was no turning back on the bet but I had not lost the match. He we simply getting ahead of the end result. I realized that the friendly competition was turning into a more violent encounter. I wanted to quit the match because I feared the adults would come out and see us doing more than wrestling but Rodger didn't care. The encounter was similar to the game of "house". On the playground in the back of the school against the wall he wanted to attempt to penetrate me before he even won the wrestling match. I said, "no" and he got upset. I left him on the playground with his erect penis.

The sleep over had already begun in the gym so it was easy to hide and ignore Rodger in the crowd. My Grandfather's class was over and it was time to go home. My parents were pretty strict when it came to sleepovers regardless of what they did not know had already happened to me.

There never seemed to be a good time to bring up the past and besides, I was still only around twelve years old. The events that were introduced into my life did not cause me to love or hate. They only cause me to analyze everything from that moment on and wonder why or when they would happen again. I felt that as long as I was not the instigator of the situation, I did not have to be the victim nor the villain. I had my Grandfather to look up to as a role model along with his sons, my father, my mother, as well as many other people in the community. Depression was settling in at a young age and GOD seemed to be on the sideline allowing everything to happen. Yet still, what I knew about GOD was good even though I had never seen or spoken to GOD.

My parents believed in GOD and regardless of their occasional fights or disagreements, they loved each other.

**6**

$\mathcal{T}$he National Youth Sports Program (NYSP) was great opportunity to meet other students from all over the country and mostly within the surrounding counties. Rust College participated in the program and it was only about nine miles away to attend it. My basketball coach took us there and brought us back everyday during the summer. There were participated in basketball, tennis, baseball, track, bowling, swimming, dance and many other activities. It was a great distraction for the summer that was positive in the community. I made a lot of friends there. One friend by the name of Mario Jones.

Mario was gay and confidently expressed his sexuality. He was from Olive Branch, MS and attended the NYSP program during the summer of my 8th grade school year. The was a teacher named Brian trying to calm the class down so he could call roll. He was call the names on the list and got to Mario's name and Mario responded. The tone of Mario's voice was very feminine and Mr. Brian offended Mario when he comment on his voice. Mario stood up and walked down the bleachers and kicked Mr. Brian in the nuts. Mr. Brian was in so much pain that he dismissed classed.

For some reason me and Mario and I struck up a conversation and became friends. We eventually convinced our mothers to allow a sleep over. All summer long we would spend the night over each others house. I eventually got a summer job at Taco Bell in Olive Branch. With my parents permission, I could work as at the age of fifteen. I worked after school and got off at closing time. On some nights I would stay over at Mario's house and simply go to school the next morning.

Mario's mom, Mrs. Nancy, was always very nice to me. She was about five foot four and kind of on the voluptuous side in appearance. She was a very religious woman.

Reminded me a lot of my mother's mother. She always had church music playing in the house. She really loved Mario and everything about him. She did not show any hatred for his sexuality.

One night I got off work and stay over at Mario's house. There were two other boys that He had had relations with that were interested in holding a conversation with me. We sat talking for about an hour or two. All of a sudden the guy asked me what made me want to be gay. It was the first time I had ever heard the word gay in regards to human behavior. I informed the boy that I was not gay because means happy. He immediately swung and punched me in the face. I kneeled on the ground and gave them warning as they ran off. I said if they were not gone by the time I got up that I was going to kill them. Mario saw everything from the garage.

I went into Mario's house and his mom asked what had happened to my eye. I told her that the boy hit me and she asked me what was I going to do about it. I said I was going to get them back the next time I saw them.

The boys were classmates of Mario's that lived in his neighborhood. I guess the boys figured I was having some type of sexual relationship with Mario at the time. That was why they assumed that I was already gay. That was still no reason for them to hit me and run off without staying to fight.

I learned a lot that summer about love, loyalty, family and somewhat betrayal. Mario and I continued too be friends but I never stayed over after work anymore from that incident.

Work at Taco Bell provided money for school supplies and clothes as well as whatever foods I liked to eat. I kind of had different tastes buds than that of my family and my father was constantly saying, "He will eat it if he gets hungry enough". That was to say they were not going to change the way they prepared their meals just to make me happy. I had to eat what was cooked and placed on the table or not eat at all. So, I guess working gave me some responsibility to self. Working did not mean I was ready to take on the world and what it had to offer. Even though my parents argued and occasionally fought, they still put food on the table and clothes on our backs. We were far from rich but we were not poor either,

Working alongside my grandfather was time consuming but necessary. I learned the value of the dollar. Working alongside my father was stressful because I knew there was no reward. I was learning from my mother that a husband is to be taken care of and he is allowed to do whatever he wanted to his wife. I was learning from my grandfather that hard work pays off. With the farm life, school work and my night time job, I was always busy. It was a distraction from being called gay, niger, dumb, and all the other derogatory comments I heard from people in the community. I was always quiet and simply focused on the future. I knew the experiences of my past were not all that GOD had in store for me.

We were in the van that took us back and forth to Rust College's National Youth Sports Program with Mr. Rayford. We were on the way home and he was making his usual stops to let off some of the kids. For some reason, Mr. Rayford's nephew had taken his wallet and Mr. Rayford blamed me. I really looked up to him because he was my coach for all my sports. It really crushed my pride because he accused me of stealing in front of everyone on the van and they all believed that I had stolen the wallet. When it came time for my stop I sprinted from the van all the way to my mother with face full of tears. After catching my breath, I explained that Mr. Rayford had accused me of stealing and I had not stolen anything.

My mother immediately told me to get in the car and we raced to meet the van at the store where it usually turned around at to go home. She confronted Mr. Rayford and he immediately said that he found out that his nephew had stolen the wallet. Mr. Rayford tried to apologize but the damage was already done. The rumors that I was a thief was already circulating around the community. I never rode in the van again to the summer programs.

All I looked forward to was getting out school and possibly making something of myself. It was the middle of the 90's. I had left what was known as junior high school. I was learning about hard work through my grandfather and my parents who provided. Life was getting up in the morning at about five a.m. and going to school. After school I would go to work and get off work at closing and make it home at around twelve midnight or later.

High school was somewhat of a rude awakening. Adjusting to the other students that I had not previously gone to school with was a lot to handle. I was sitting in the cafeteria eating when a girl asked why I sat the way I was sitting. I didn't know I was supposed to maintain a certain posture while eating but I didn't look cool in the way that I was sitting to her. Needless to say, I adjusted myself at the table and she began to laugh at me and caused all the other students to laugh and notice me. It was one of the most uncomfortable feelings in my freshman year,

I eventually adjusted to the treatment I was receiving and found a way to fit in with the other students. I joined the track at our high school. I was doing anything to avoid having free time because free time meant that I would have to help clean the school after hours with Charles.

I would still talk to Mario and on the phone one night I met Mr. Benford. He was an ex-military nurse who worked part-time for a suicide prevention hotline. We were on a three way phone call and Mr. Benford invited me over to his house for a birthday party with my mother's permission. I went to the birthday party and enjoyed the treatment of Mr. Benford that I wanted to stay with them and finish the remainder of my high school years in Memphis at Central High School. Mr. Benford had a roommate by the name of Christopher. They were both gay. They treated me like I was a son or younger brother. They were good male role models as far as keeping a stable job and staying out of jail. Jail was one of the many options in life I was trying to avoid.

There was not many people my age to play with so I would always find a way to convince my mother to allow me to stay the weekend over Mr. Benford's just so I could say I was in the the city. She would eventually agree because she knew I wanted to be out of the way. Those weekends went by fast and they help the high school years go by even faster. Before I knew it I was in summer of the year before graduating,

I got my mother to sign a permission slip allow Mr. Benford guardianship over me during my senior year. I had already been absent from school at Byhalia High for beginning of the school year because I was waiting for classes to begin at Central High in Memphis, TN. I was sitting in my classroom at Central on the first day of school and the policeman came in and ask me to come with him. I grabbed my things and went with the officer to the principal's office. They were classifying me as a runaway.

My father had become upset with the thought of me switching schools that he beat my mother to make her change her mind on giving me consent to change schools. The principal said that I had to be withdrawn from Central High immediately and return to Byhalia or Mr. Benford would be charged with kidnapping. There was nothing we could do.

When I returned to Byhalia High everyone laughed and joked about me missing school. I was informed by the principal that in order to graduate I could not miss any days from school since I had already missed twenty days of school. I said that I understood and had no intentions of failing simply because of attendance.

# 7

Charles and I only became more distant because he thought I was trying to give up on school and I was simply trying to attend a bigger school. I felt as though most of my parents arguments was about me but it was honest because Charles had a severe drug and alcohol problem. I had learn to not ask for much or do without.

Sports was always a great distraction or outlet from what was going on in my immediate surroundings. Farm life was hard work and I loved the thought of staying in shape while working on the land, It was a beautiful way to stay connected to what I felt and knew about GOD.

GOD seemed to be sitting on the sideline allowing everything to happen. Rust college was a HBCU school that I loved going to during the summers. Since my incident with Mr. Rayford I had outgrown NYSP and moved on to a program called Upward Bound and HCOP. These programs were based on GPA. They offered a stipend and possible scholarship if you did well. We were taken on field trips to colleges and universities all over the country throughout the summer and lived and attend classes on campus at Rust College that prepared us for college life. It was a wonderful opportunity.

I learned that summer during the orientation process that I had acquired an STD from my childhood molestations so I was given penicillin to cure it. However the damage had been done.

After taking all the required shots and doing the paperwork I attended the Health Care Occupational Program at Rust College in 1995. I made a lot of friends with students from all over the state of Mississippi. Attending that program I acquired a love for medicine and traveling the country. I saw so much about the country and the world that there was no way Mississippi was all that GOD had to offer.

It was always my name that was haunting me. Just the simple action of being force to write it differently put so many obstacles in my future. Legally, I was a Porter or a Moore. It was a life and a reality I was learning to live with,

You cannot change a birth certificate, you can only change a name. It was getting close to graduation. I had a cheerleading scholarship to Mississippi State University. I was the first male cheerleader at my high school. I chose to go to MSU because it was far enough away but close enough for emergency. I was a huge campus and I figure I would study in the field of science after attend the HCOP program at Rust College. I knew I didn't see myself doing a job that had me standing or sitting in one place.

Mr. Benford thought that I should take a break from school and just go later because school was all I ever did. I was determined to get out of my parents' house and on with life on my own terms. I was trying to avoid major depression by staying as busy as possible.

Graduation was in May of 1996. It was held at Rust College in the gymnasium. We threw our hats high and shed our tears and thought if we would ever see each other again. I was set off for Mississippi State in Starkville Mississippi.

I got to the huge campus with my parents dropping off at the freshman's dormitory. It was beautiful. The dorm counselor greeted me at the entrance to the door and led me to my room. My mom did her look over of the room and ask if I was going to be okay. I said yes. She sat my bag down and gave me a big hug and said, "Call me if you need anything". She walked down the hallway and out of the building. All the boys whistling as she walked by them. My mother looked very young.

This was my first taste of freedom but I cried with worry as my mother left. As I walked back into the dormitory my roommate was waiting at the door. His name was Shakobee. He reintroduced himself and said he was from Meridian, MS. I said, "Oh, that's just right down the road". He replied, "Yeah".

I got settled into the dorm pretty fast and made lots of friends. College life was a completely different atmosphere from high school. It was a larger crowd and easy go unseen if you want to. I didn't have much. I only had the clothes that I had taken care of over the school years and about 20 dollars to my name. I was waiting for the financial aid check that would come during the first semester's end.

I was able to get food stamps because of my income. I ate in the school cafeteria and got a job a the Taco Bell in the student union. The money from my scholarship had already been applied to my tuition so I had no money for books unless I took out a student loan.

Cheerleading was a stressful routine. We practiced in the mornings, afternoons, and evenings.

I was in Cheerleading practice learning how to do a flip when one of the most beautiful girls I had ever seen came into the gymnasium. In the middle of my flip I saw her walk through the door. In my landing I was still holding my feet and stepped on my thumb. She was just that beautiful. Her name was Michelle.

I was still very attracted to the opposite sex and was simply glad to be away from everyone that seemed to be related to me. I was on the verge of experiencing some form of a normal life.

I was walking on campus near the administration building when I saw two girls coming.

They were the high yellow light skinned type. They had log hair and just as beautiful as Michelle. They wee walking down the sidewalk near the build where we went to meet our guidance counselor. I made my way over to the sidewalk they were on just so I would get the chance to greet them.

As I walk up on them they were talking and laughing. I greeted them with a hello and they said nothing as if they didn't hear me so I spoke again.

I got the attention of Divian Conner and Teresa Taylor. They were first cousins. Divian was studying psychology and Teresa was studying Elementary Education. I gave them the ice breaker line of "I thought you two were stuck up." Not that I had a chance of being with one of them.

They asked me why I thought they were stuck up. I said "Because you are so beautiful and usually pretty girls are stuck up". They were far from stuck up because they showed appreciation to the compliment of being pretty. I offered to carry their books as we were all going to the guidance counselor,

I was informed of all the classes I would have for the first semester and the books that I would need. I found out that I couldn't afford any books without taking out a student loan,

I had to attend classes without any books until my financial aid arrived.

My father thought it was best I survive on my own so he only gave me twenty dollars to begin the semester. I used the money to buy paper so that I could take notes. It was going to be two weeks before I received my first check from TacoBell in the student union.

A few weeks had passed and I had gotten settled into campus. There was a block party near the student union. A few of my classmates from high school had chosen to go the Mississippi State University so there were a few familiar faces. I saw Michelle standing and talking with a few other girls so I got enough nerve to strike up a conversation. She was even more beautiful close up and in person. I had only seen her at cheerleading practice since she was trying out for the pompom squad. In our conversation I found out that she was only 16 and already in college. He mother had passed away so she too was on her own and paying for her own education. We continued to talk and found out that we made each other laugh. We exchanged information and began a friendship immediately. I asked her to dance and she agreed. She wasn't a great dancer as she quickly admitted, but we danced during the entire event. The block party ended and we went to our dorms.

A few weeks had passed and I was getting more stressed with classes and figuring out how to pay for school. In high school I had spoken to an Army recruiter but I decided to go to college. I was walking around the student union and a Navy recruiter approached me. It was a week before the end of the first semester ended; December 19th. The recruiter explained all the benefits and opportunities that the Navy had to offer. All I had was a partial scholarship and a part-time job at TacoBell. The recruiter asked me what score I made on the ASVAB test. He said I qualified for the Navy if I could make a score of ten points higher. I retook the test and made the high score. I signed to go the Navy and leave for bootcamp on December 26, 1996.

It had been a few days since I seen Michelle, Divian or Teresa or any of my other friends that I made in such short time. When I saw Michelle she was walking around the track field looking depressed. When I made it to her I ask her what was wrong. She quickly replied, "I'm pregnant". I immediately said, "The school has a day care and your mother would be happy if you stayed in school." I finished with the statement, "I've signed up to go into the Navy and whatever help I can offer, I will, if you stay in school. We continued walking around the track field and made promises to each other in support of her staying in school and also in support of me taking charge of my life a joining the military. We were both going down uncertain roads. I knew I was only trying to be a friend and not give up.

$\mathcal{M}$y mother was not surprised that I had joined the military. She was a little upset that I left immediately the day after Christmas. I at least wanted to spend the holidays before bootcamp. I was ready to see what the Navy had to offer. I knew it was a steady job and I would have structure and benefits with advancement opportunity. I also knew that by signing to serve the my country, I was signing to risk my life to do so.

I made it to Ohara Airport in Illinois. It was early in the morning around three o'clock. They immediately shaved our heads and completed our shots and paperwork to get checked into bootcamp. I discovered that I was assigned to the aviation department instead of the medical department. They said the medical department was full and if I really wanted the medical department, I would have to cross-train from aviation to medical in my free time. It was too late to back out.

Bootcamp was hard. I had two tough RDCs, Recruit Division Commanders; one male and one the other a female. There were not many women in the Navy at the time, but my female Senior Chief Petty Officer was tough. I was doing pretty well in bootcamp and had earned the privilege of rookie Sunday. Rookie Sunday was freedom to go to church and talk on the phone on Sundays. I was talking to my mother whom I had not spoken to for weeks. She said my father had hit her again with a pipe while they were out in public. I was furious as usual. But there was nothing I could do because she loved him. I asked to speak with my father. She gave him the phone and for the first time I told him that I would hurt him if he continued to put his hands on my mother.

There was not much I could really do to protect my mother as I had promised to never raise my hand to Charles. My mother would always say "Don't hate people, hate their ways".

I was over a thousand miles away I a military that was full of discrimination and racism.

However, the military had more promise and opportunity than what my Homelife had to offer.

All I could do was maintain focus.

I had received orders to report to the flight deck of the USS Eisenhower CVN 69, a nuclear powered aircraft carrier in Norfolk, Virginia. I figured I would work on my medical career while working on the flight deck in my free time, which was hard to come by working sixteen hour days.

Life on the flight deck was hard and fast paced. I had to pay attention to detail or risk being killed. Work during the day was just as difficult as work during the night. We slept directly under the flight deck so you needed earplugs while you slept. The ship was so big in size that I could barely feel the movement. The flight deck was over

332 meters (1089 ft long). It housed over 85 aircraft and over 3000 personnel at one time. It is a magnificent ship.

I immediately adjusted to flight deck life. I got into working out and formed a basketball team on the ship. In my free time I would work on the medical ward during OJT (on the job training) as a hospital corpsman so I could eventually leave the flight deck and work in medicine.

I was walking in the cafeteria when I met Sunny Cedric. Cedric was noticeably feminine but he worked in a different department of the ship as a mechanic. We quickly became friends and he informed me that he was gay. President Clinton had enacted the "Don't Ask, Don't Tell" Act, but I was still afraid to discuss sexuality due to fear of being dishonorably discharged. Nevertheless, it was understood between the two of us. Cedric was from Washington, DC. Every weekend that we had off work, we would drive up to DC and he would visit his family. I would drive over to Baltimore to visit my cousin and his lover. A year had gone by pretty fast and it was the year 1997.

I was spending time with Cedric and making the best of life. At least we had something in common in regards to our lifestyles. I had made friend with two other girls, Kelly and Nikki. Kelly reminded me of Jada Pinkett. Nikki reminded me of Pamela Anderson. They were both beautiful. Kelly was from Indiana and Nikki was from Arkansas. They were in bootcamp together and had formed a romantic relationship. Kelly worked on the flight deck with me and Nikki was on a ship called the Emory S. Land. It was a sub-tender.

It was hard work on the flight deck. Not paying attention could cost you your life. It was an added stress to the reality of life. I was still finding out who I was while being a part of a military that would kick me out if I chose to behave in a homosexual manner. Whatever free time we had it went to a second job off the ship or simply getting away on the days we did not have duty.

I had decided that if I was going to stay in the military I would aim for the highest rank. I planned to become a flight deck medical officer in order to make a difference in the Navy. I guess I was ambitious.

We were about to go on our first Mediterranean cruise. It was the first time I was leaving the country. I was doing pretty good in my training and had mad a few friends on the flight deck and throughout the ship. I was supervising a few new shipmates that had just graduated bootcamp and the Aviation Training Department when Robert came onboard the ship. He flew in on a cod when we were about to go across the equator. He was tall and dark and very funny. He was from St. Louis.

I was given the title of flight deck liaison. I was the one who met and greeted all new flight deck personnel and showed them around the ship. I had become pretty popular on the flight deck and had gotten the nickname of "Big Sexy" because of the way I looked and the fact that I was weighing around 225 pounds. I was hit on by both male and female. I was too focused on my Naval career than to get involve in a relationship. My friends would call me a "goodie two shoes".

Our ship had pulled in to Anatolya, Turkey. We were schedule to be there for five days. The rules of the land were very strict. We were ordered to stay close to the ship due to the laws of Turkey. The port did have a tourist attraction of the Sheraton Hotel where most of the sailors went to relax.

It felt good to swim in the water. I met Cedric at the pool because we were not going to risk going inland and being subject or victim to the laws of Turkey. Cedric was still the only friend that I felt the most comfortable with on the ship. Since Robert and I worked together, he wanted to hang out after work so he decided to meet me at the pool. Robert was a little bit older than me and already had children of his own. He joined the Navy for the same reason as most do…. Opportunity.

We had been sitting by the pool for a few hours. Ine decided to go and talk to one his coworkers from his department who he saw at the pool. Robert and I were alone and started talking about family life and work and reasons for joining the military. We talked for about an hour before we noticed Cedric had not returned. We became closer in our conversation.

For some reason, Robert mentioned that he had tuberculosis. He said it caused him to have difficulty breathing and very bad chest and body aches, but he managed to deal with it and join the Navy. We got into the pool and tried to cool off from the sun. The pool had a slide and a bar that served alcoholic beverages. I was not old enough to drink.

After a few minutes in the water, Robert began to have some sort of reaction to swimming. He said it felt like he was having a stroke so I got we got out the water and I told him to lay still on his back for a few minutes until the symptoms wore off, I went to get a glass of ice to help keep him cool. When I returned, he thanked me for bringing him the ice to eat. He seemed impressed with my concern for him so he kind of began to flirt.

I was still operating under the rule of "Don't Ask, Don't Tell". In the middle of what I thought was a medical emergency, he chose to cross the lines of flirting with a coworker. Since I had submitted an application to Officer Candidate School, I had no intention of crossing the lines of fraternization, not to mention I didn't know if he was actually flirting or simply talking and it seemed like flirtation.

Cedric returned and saw me hovering over Robert next to the pool and asked what was wrong. I informed Cedric that Robert was have a reaction to the pool and the hot sun so we were going to go back to the ship. Cedric noticed that Robert and I had formed a bond that was more than just friends. Robert and I returned to the ship where we live, worked, and slept together in the same space. He was actually flirting and informed me that his mother had friends who were gay. As he insisted he was not gay. And insisted that I had never acted on and advancement towards a man.

We continued to keep our friendship strictly professional. We always saw each other on the flight deck and every time the ship hit a port, we were together.....as friends.

We were sitting in the cafeteria and there was an event call rookie Sunday on the ship.

The ship would serve ice cream and crab legs, crawfish and shrimp and steak. Everyone would come to eat and pig out on the food. Different departments would merge together and new friendships would form.

We had been at sea for well over a month and our next port was going to be Korfu, Greece. The cafeteria was full and there was nowhere to sit and I saw a girl with a short haircut looking kind of tomboyish. It was the only place to sit so I sat next to her at the end of the long table. He last name was Ross and she called herself "Smiley". She said she was from Texas and worked in the Seaman Department as a repairman. Just like Robert and I, she had joined the Navy for the opportunity as well.

We sat there talking and we found out we had basketball in common and she like to drive fast. She and my mother were born in the same month so that was enough for me to bond with her. We sat there in the crowded cafeteria people watching. I noticed that she was kind of buff for a girl and she hadn't mentioned anything about a boy in our conversation, Since we didn't work together we decided to meet in the Hangar Deck of the ship and play basketball together. Our work schedule was different since we worked in different departments so we set days to work out together as well.

Robert came down and saw me talking to Ross, He made his way to the table we were sitting at and sat beside me. I introduced him to Ross. The quickly became friends. Then Ringo came down. He was from St. Louis just like Robert. We all sat there and became closer and share funny stories about home life and what we loved and hated about the military life. Eventually, Ine came to cafeteria and joined us at the table. At that moment, it was obvious that me and Ine were gay friends and the group had no problems.

We continued talking until the food was gone and it was time to go to bed, The ship could easily put you to sleep as it swayed through the water. Ringo, Robert and I went to our birthings where we slept, Cedric went to his department and Ross went to her department.

It was only a few days before we made it to Korfu, Greece.

I was missing home, the United States, Tuggle and Nikki,

I had left my car with Kelly and Nikki back at home before the ship left. It was a Mazda Protege. Before leaving Norfolk I had gone to a club and met a guy named Jackson who was a civilian and we had been intimate. He was planning on moving to a new apartment and need to use my car so I arranged for him to pick up my car from Nikki and Kelly. Jackson came to pick up my car and I received a letter from Nikki saying at Jackson had not returned my car. There was nothing I could do but call the police from the ship.

I called home and spoke with my mom and she seemed well. There had not been a fight nor and argument in over a year but she said Charles's health was not doing so well. I informed her that my car had possibly been stolen and it was because I had trusted another human being... once again. She replied, "Put that in GOD's hands". I had not heard those words in a long time. It is like you forgive someone even though they have not asked for forgiveness. So I put the loss of my car in the hands of GOD because I could not do anything from halfway around the world. Besides the police would not even classify the car as stolen since I left my keys in the hands of another person. The police labeled it as "unauthorized use".

Back on the ship we were about to pull into the Port of Korfu, Greece. I had become really close to my new friends since the were now my family away from family. I was a huge ship with something always going on, yet, it was easy to become depressed. After being seen with my new friends and a sense of family we had become the talk of the ship... so to speak. People had begun to make rumors regarding sexuality and lifestyle so I would accidentally overhear them on the ship talking amongst each other. It was beginning to be like high school all over again. There was nowhere to run on the massive ship.

The ship pulled into the Port of Korfu, Greece. It was a majestic site along the mountainside. The people were beautiful. We were scheduled to be there for five days. In port the duties on the flight deck were lightened because no jets could fly. The Port of Korfu was a friendly port visit. We had more time to relax.

The first thing most of the sailors did was check into a hotel room so we could take a hot tub bath. It was nice to soak in a hot tub of water and relax the muscles. Robert wanted to get a room with me so Cedric got a room with one of the girls we had made friends with while at sea, It was a beautiful hotel by the seaside. Since we were operating within the laws of Greece, the legal age was sixteen and as the saying goes, "When in Rome, do as the Romans do." Well, we were close enough.

Later in the day the group decided to meet up an go to a toga party. The music was blasting and the drinks were going around. I was still a minor in the states but now I was of legal age to drink. I felt like an adult and was not planning to get drunk nor drive anywhere.

We all were having so much fun dancing and mingling with the natives. The night was going long. Robert had had a bit too much to drink. We were sitting at the table with our drinks talking about his girlfriend and his children and what he was wanting to do for her with his earnings. I applauded his act to take care of her and his family. As we sit and talk in the loud music his two front teeth popped out and fell into the beer mug. We laughed so hard because I too was feeling the liquor. I immediately reached into the mug and gave him back his teeth and he put them back in his mouth as we continued laughing it off. He said that he was feeling body pain and wanted to go to the room. I handed him the key but he wanted me to go to the room with him. I didn't see why but I went along anyway.

Early in the day we had gone shopping and purchase some playing cards that had some adult pictures on them, As we got to the room Robert asked me if I knew how to give a massage. I said yes, not knowing his intentions. I guess the long months at sea had caused him to have uncontrollable urges. I walked in behind him and he went to his bed and laid down immediately. I went to my bed and he said, "I thought you were going to give me a massage". I said, "You only asked if I knew how to give a massage". The room got completely silent for about three minutes. I said, "I have seven Aunts on my mom's side and I am only used to giving them massages". He said, "It should be the same". I didn't think too much into it. I said, "I was molested and I am not use to touching men". He said, "Nothing is going happen that you don't want to." He said, "I only want a massage for my body pain because it helps to sooth the symptoms of Tuberculosis." I said, "Okay, I will do it".

I left my bed and went to Robert bed. He began to undress. I overreacted and asked "What are you doing". He said, "Calm down, it's just a massage". He undressed down to his underwear. It was different from bootcamp where you are in the shower with over 100 men completely naked. This time there was no supervision, He laid on his stomach on the bed so I could do his back first.

I began rubbing his body and felt the heat. He said, "Massage harder". I said, "Okay, just let me know if I hurt you".

He said, "I'm man enough to handle it". I continued massaging.

I finished massaging the back of Robert and I said, "Okay. Turn over". Robert hesitated and I asked him what was wrong, He immediately said, "This has never happened to me". I said, "what are you talking about". He immediately flipped over as I was straddling his back, His penis was rock hard, I jumped back a bagged up against the wall.

He said, "What's wrong". I said, "Are you okay, I thought you said nothing was going to happen that I didn't want". He said, "Nothing has happened yet". He got up from his bed and walked towards me. I said, "I'm trying to become an officer and I don't want to get kicked out for fraternization. He said, "But, you are not an officer yet." He walked closer to me and I was against the wall, He place his hands on the wall and was directly in front of me with a hard penis. He said, "I've never been with a man before and I have a girlfriend but we are separated". I said, "What is that supposed to mean to me". He kissed me and I kissed him back. In that moment all my past resurfaced. This time it was a different encounter.

Robert grabbed my hands and walked me to his bed. I asked,

"What about the other side of his body?" He said, "Do what you are comfortable with". I said, "I've never been comfortable". He was laying there with a massive penis and wanting me to play the role of the woman. We made love until the sunrise.

Cedric saw me the next morning at the breakfast bar of the hotel. It had only been one day on land with Robert and Cedric already was suspicious. Robert and I was passed the initial "Don't Ask, Don't Tell."

I played dumb but Cedric knew something had happened. The days went by in Greece and we were on to the next port in Spain. I didn't believe that Robert had I were a couple because of one sexual encounter and we still had to work alongside each other and live with the secret of being intimate with each other. We were at sea for another month before we made it to Spain. The port was much different from Greece. It was dirty. The country seemed very poor at the time.

## 9

$\mathcal{T}$he ship made it to Spain during Cinco De Mayo. I phoned back to talk to Michelle who was still in school at Mississippi State University. She was about to give birth to Jeshaun, my Godson. It was rumored that Jeshaun was my biological child. So she named him after me.

I remember talking on the phone just before she was about to go into labor, I used the phones at the pier in Spain where the ship was docked. I was so happy that she wanted me to be a Godfather. I gave me great honor. I was more proud that she decided to stay in school after our conversation walking around the track field before I joined the Navy. Our conversation was not long because she had just taken medication for labor.

Robert found me near the phones and saw my excitement. I was running around like I was about to be a father, He was using the phones as well to talk to the mother of his children. He wanted to know If I wanted to go and shoot basketball at the set up near the pier. I said yes.

Everyone was there to shoot basketball. It seemed like everyone from the ship was there. We shot ball for a few hours in the blistering sun. We returned to the ship and decided to go to one of the local bars in town that was in the "red light district". Well… we thought it was a bar.

We got inside and the women were all walking along in bedtime clothes. Sexy night wear. The place was a whore house, yet, a lot of the sailors were there; officers and enlisted alike.

I quickly learned that Robert was not going to belong to me. We sat in the club for a few minutes and order a few drinks and a woman came up to Robert and whispered something into his ear and he was gone for about an hour and a half. I was only left to assume. Downstairs in the first floor was like a bar and night club. Upstairs there were rooms that people could go to have sex with the women. I had too much respect for my mother to do anything with the women there. Besides I was still deciding on what I wanted in life. I did not want to cause more frustration by misleading a woman if women were not what I really wanted. So I stayed sitting by the bar, turning down every woman that came to make a sexual advance.

Ringo saw my frustration and ask what was wrong with me. Before long, he started to assume that I was upset about something between Robert and I since the three of us worked in the same division. All of a sudden, Robert reappeared and saw my frustration. I knew we had not come to an agreement of being a couple but I was not discussed or understood what kind of relationship we were forming. Nevertheless, we all were connected.

It wasn't long before we were going to be returning to the states. President Clinton was in office and we were going to war in Kosovo,

There was nothing we could do about it, Then out of nowhere, a sailor was killed by two of his coworkers for being gay. The rumors were starting on the ship regarding my sexuality and Robert and I were spending much more time with each other. Whenever you saw me, you would see him.

A few other of my friends were beginning to come out of the closet and the military was allowing those who were gay to get out of the military with an honorable discharge if they came forward. I was not ready to do so because I had never been the initiator of a sexual advance so I was deciding on how much of the gay lifestyle I was apart of. I had only been molested and Robert was the first mutual encounter where I was willing and wanting.

Our next port visit was Naples, Italy. Ross, Cedric and I had become like best friends. Yet we knew that if it wasn't for joining the Navy, we never would have met each other. We had five days in Naples, Italy. The city was full of cathedrals and castles. We were not far from Pompeii so I decided to go alone on a train ride to visit the ruins and take pictures. I had to clear my head. Life was unfolding once again and I wanted to be alone with GOD.

I took lots of pictures of the statues and taverns and cliffs along the coast line. I was talking to one of the natives on the train and passed my train stop at the ruins of Pompeii and ended up traveling to Sorrento, Italy. I walked around taking pictures and learning the language. I stopped and bought a glass of Ferreira wine and enjoy an Italian croissant along the mountainside restaurant. I decided I would stop by the ruins on the way back to the ship.

I was amazed to see the aftermath of the volcanic eruption had produce a Venus fly trap near the tourist attraction. At the fly trap, a black widow had built its web directly above the jaws of the plant. As if they were working together.

I had been gone mostly all day since I had no duty. After the events of Spain, I was wondering what would be the nature of Robert and my relationship once we returned to the states. I knew I was growing deep feelings for him and I didn't not want to confuse my feeling of commitment with it being a simple work fling.

I returned to the ship and informed my friend of where they could go since they had not left the ship yet. Naples was a quiet port visit. Paris was a three hour train ride away and Sorrento was only thirty minutes. The next day I was off work, so, I planned to go to see the Eiffel Tower. I returned to the ship to meet with friends and let them know of the place I had seen in case they wanted to see for themselves.

The next day I had duty. It had been over a month and a half since Robert and I had discussed our moment in Greece. We were both consenting adults. I had not spoken to anyone else about our involvement with each other because of "Don't Ask, Don't Tell".

We only had about two more days in Italy. My friends and I planned to hang out in Paris for the day. It was only a 3 hour train ride. The city was beautiful but full of ways to get into trouble. So we stuck together. it was the entire group. Ringo, Cedric, Ross, Robert and I plus a few other coworkers that wanted to come along. We were walking through the city and shopping for things to send home to our loved ones. We were happy to be with each other even though we came from different backgrounds.

We had been walking through the city for hours. All of a sudden a group of people from Italy came riding by on motorcycles. One of them got close to us at the corner of the sidewalk and spit on me. I immediately tried to knock them off their bike because it upset me but Owen grabbed my arm before I could swing. Either way, I would have been in serious trouble if the matter would have escalated into a legal matter in Italy. I immediately wanted to return to the ship and

the group agreed. We caught the train back to Naples and stay close
to the ship until we departed from Naples, Italy.

We were back at sea with orders to go to Kosovo for war. I
was twenty years old and on the other side of the world. Life hand
unfolded completely. We only had about two more months at sea
and there was no turning back from Kosovo. I called home and
spoke with my mom and let her know that our ship was going to
Kosovo. She cried a little and the conversation went back to normal.
It was a quick conversation because someone else was waiting to
use the phone.

We were in the middle of the war. Our ship was fully stocked
with jets and missiles and ready to launch. I knew I was a part of
what was about to be the death of civilians. I had been in the Navy
three years and about to be a part of my first war. All of a sudden,
President Clinton order us to stand down. Our ship didn't launch the
missiles. I was pleased that I didn't have to be a part of destruction,
however I was deciding to end my naval career due to harassment
from coworkers and the thought of someone trying to kill me for
being gay. I didn't see a life in the military because the laws were
not allowing it.

The ship was to return to the shipyards in Portsmouth, Virginia.
We were going to make it back and go in to repair from the war and
the six months that we were at sea. I did not know what was going
to be the nature of Robert and my relationship once we returned to
the states. I remained focus on the flight deck and awaited the return
to the states. I was relieved that we were not going to war so I would
not have the memory.

We made it back to Norfolk, Virginia. The first thing I did was
contact the police regarding my Mazda Protégé. Jackson had left my
car abandoned in a church parking lot. It was stripped down to the

to the rotors. My intentions of doing a good deed in letting someone use my car had taught me a valuable lesson on trust. Nevertheless, I searched for a new car because the car seemed too expensive to repair. I prepared to return home to Mississippi to visit my mother on leave of duty. It had been almost 2 years since I had been home.

The ship went to Portsmouth, Virginia for repairs. My application for Officer Candidates School was under review and I had completed the training I needed to cross over from the flight deck to the medical department. All my plans seemed to be going well. Ross and I got part-time jobs at H&R Block. Since the ship was in repair, we had more free time. We needed the extra money. Life on the ship was different when we were docked in the states. It was almost like we were civilian with a regular eight hour job. The rumors of our sexuality began to surface and it was becoming stressful and hostile to work amongst those whom had strong feeling about sexuality and the way someone behaved. Some sailors were being kicked out for their sexuality, some were being kicked out for disorderly conduct. Ross came to me and confessed of her sexuality and wanted to go the Washington D.C. to hang out with Ine and I. We all needed to get away from the ship. We were all having issues with our coworkers. Robert and I were still figuring out where we stood in our relationship. We took leave for two weeks so we could think about our Naval careers. We all knew that without the Navy we would be returning to the life we left when joining. None of us wanted to return to those circumstances.

We made it to Washington D.C. and dropped Cedric off at his brother's house. Ross and I went on to Baltimore and were going to stay with my cousin who was gay. My cousin had a lover who served in the Coast Guard at the time. I got to my cousin's house and hid under his bed so I could surprise him. His lover kept the secret.

When my cousin got home I grabbed his leg from under his bed and scared the shit out of him. We laughed it off and decided to go down to the harbor for dinner. It had been over fifteen yrs since I had seen my cousin. He was full of energy. He was happy to have someone come to visit him. He was even more happy that I was growing up to be gay and proudly serving in the military. He said, "It's good you are trying to make something out of yourself... Shaun". Shilonda, as he would joke by giving me a feminine name. I would just laugh it off even though the feminine name frustrated me. I felt very masculine.

My cousin made Ross and I feel at home. We were going to be staying with him for the two week that we were on leave. We were making the biggest decision of our life.

Ross and I decided to go out to the club in Baltimore with my cousin. He was happy to show us the lifestyle of Baltimore night life. We made it to the club and went straight for the dance floor. We were both great dancers. A girl named Maria quickly came over and wanted to dance with Ross. She and the girl quickly hit it off and exchanged numbers. I was too shy to dance with anyone and was honestly try to see where my relationship with Robert was going to go, We danced the night away and decide to go back to Maria's house. She introduced us to her best friends Bill and Lamont.

It was winter time and a blizzard was coming. We got snowed in at Maria's house. We were stuck there about five days. We had so much fun. Maria and Ross got more acquainted.

The weather broke and I was able to make it to my cousin's apartment. Ross decided to stay behind with Maria and spend more time with her. I was spending time with my cousin and he became worried that was doing something wrong because I was away from the ship too long. I had to explain to him that I was on leave and everything was perfectly fine. I decided to go to D.C to spend some time with Cedric. We only had about five more days on leave and the weather was getting worse again. I hung out with Cedric about two days and returned to my cousin's apartment and waited for the weather to subside.

I decided to go for a walk to get a work out. I was walking along the sidewalk when I saw a guy starring at me. I had never been starred at like that before. I turned around and asked the guy why was he looking at me like that. To my surprise, he said, "You are fine as hell". I didn't know what to say. He insisted that we hang out together. I called my cousin and let him know that I met someone while walking. My cousin said I could go back to his apartment if I wanted to. So the guy named T and I went back to my cousin's apartment. My cousin was not going to be home for a few hours so we decided to get to know each other better. Before long we found ourselves being intimate. I had not made any promises to Robert and he seemed to be doing whatever he wanted. So I felt free to enjoy the moment with T.

The next day I told my cousin all about my moment with T. After a few details of the encounter my cousin began to laugh. He laughed so hard that I was becoming frustrated.

My cousin informed me that he too had. Been intimate with T. I began to laugh with him.

We both said, "It's a small world".

I went back over to Maria's house. Ross seemed to be in love. We both had run out of money and had none to get gas to return to Norfolk. I had used the last of my money. I was in the car with Bill and Lamont and too embarrassed to ask anyone for money. Bill and Lamont talked me into driving into a gas station that was pump before you pay. We were in Ross's car. It was a dark green Honda Elantra. I didn't know that Bill had gone into the store and only bought a few snacks. We filled the car up with gas. After a few minutes at the pump, Bill got back into the car and said I'm done filling up, you can drive off. I didn't bother to ask if he had paid for the gas.

We got back to Maria's house and Ross looked at me and asked how did I pay for the gas. I said Bill took care of it. That was the end of discussion. Ross was in pain. We had to get back to the ship. We had already been gone too long due to the weather,

We didn't have to pick up Cedric in D.C. because he had purchased a car and driven back himself. We got back to the ship and returned to our departments. Ross and I were both in trouble but were shown lenience due to the weather being able to be proven. The police came to the ship regarding Ross's car being recorded leaving the gas station. The had a description but Ross told them that she was in the hospital. The police only wanted for the price of the gas to be paid. Bill had paid for the majority of the gas at the pump and left a balance at the station. Ross said that she didn't know who was driving the car. After she informed me of what the police said, I paid her for the gas. We were both lucky that was all that was required.

## 10

*M*aria came down to Norfolk from Baltimore to visit Ross. The
had fallen deeply in love, so it seemed. We were planning to come
forward and inform our departments of our sexuality so we could exit
the military, We just didn't want a dishonorable discharge, We didn't
want to give up on what we had worked for, but the threat of being
harmed by our coworkers was on the rise, More sailors were coming
forward and the military was issuing Honorable Discharges, There
seemed to be some light at the end of the tunnel,

I was walking on the ship when I overheard some coworkers
discussing my sexuality and what should be done to me, They were
making jokes about how Robert and I were always seen together, I
walked around the corner and heard a loud rumbling sound, Robert
and another guy were fighting, The guys had been discussing my
sexuality and were accusing Robert of being gay, Robert seemed to
have won the fight but he was thrown in the brig. He was going to
be in military jail for thirty days for bad behavior. Life changed in

that instant. I no longer felt safe amongst my coworkers and decided to report what I had heard to my commanding officers. They placed me on suicide watch and isolated me from the division for protection.

Ross was being harassed in her department and so was Cedric. Ross decided to come forward with her sexuality and report the harassment of her coworkers as well. I was giving up on my application to Officer's Candidate School. Even though the military had a lot to offer, at the moment I didn't feel safe amongst my coworkers.

I decided to leave the ship for my safety and so did Ross. We both missed ships movement and were gone twenty-eight days. When I got back to the ship I was to report to Captain's Mass. My entire department was under investigation and once again I was shown leniency because of my outstanding record for the past three years. I was offered the opportunity to transfer to a different ship but I decided that I was done with my military career due to safety reasons. It was going to take about two weeks to process my paperwork.

I was discharged from the Navy on November 19th, 1999. Even though I received an honorable discharge, misconduct was still typed on my DD214. It followed me on every job application that I applied for. It was haunting. I began to regret my decision to exit the military. I could have stayed in and made a difference. I could have dealt with my coworkers and the stress of my sexuality like most that had chosen to stay behind.

Robert was still in the brig. Ross had been discharged and returned to Texas. I returned to Mississippi but got a job in Memphis at MCI. It was a start. I decided I had outgrown my hometown of Holly Springs and Como, so I move to Memphis to be closer to my job. After the last conversation of Robert and I, I figured I would never see him again.

I returned to hanging out with Mario and going to go visit

Michelle and Jeshaun often. For the most part, life was like I never left home. Once again I was truly on my own. I got an apartment in downtown Memphis at the 99 Towers Apartments. It was overlooking the Mississippi River. I refused to go back to living with my parents. I wanted them to know that I could take care of myself. I also wanted to be a child that grew up to give back to his parents as often as I could.

On occasion, Mario would come to visit me at my apartment. I was going into a deep depression. I felt like I was failing myself and all my dreams of becoming a doctor was seeping through some invisible crack in existence. I had lost contact with my Navy friends and life was once again, all work and no play. It was a strict nine to five at MCI.

I was using my parents car to go back and forth to work when I went through a yellow light and the police pulled me over saying that I had run the red light. What could I do. Now I was in the system of going to court. I ended up loosing my job at MCI due to having to go to court so often. I went back to working for Taco Bell as an Assistant General Manager. That lasted for a while until injuries from the military interfered with my duties at Taco Bell. I could not do a job where I had to stand in one place for a long period of time. Eventually, I gave Taco Bell my two weeks notice and attempted going to school.

I was in school and the cost of school became too expensive to continue. I withdrew and went back to working. I had no friends and it seemed like no one to talk to. I was completely depressed but too proud to seek medical help or admit it.

I eventually went to jail for missing court. I was not in the system. I called my grandfather and he and my mother came to bail me out of jail. That was when I me Pamela Pollard, a bails bondsman.

She was short and had a coke bottle shape. Her complexion was very fair, high yellow skin tone. Most guy would call her a "red bone". As I waited for my parents to arrive from Mississippi to pick me up from jail, Pamela and I became good friends and exchanged numbers. She listened to my story and understood that I chose to go to work over going to court, so, that was the reason I was arrested for a warrant.

I began hanging with Pamela to stay out of trouble until I found another job. I lost my apartment at 99 Towers and eventually moved into The Claridge House Apartments on Madison Avenue in downtown Memphis. I moved into the apartments and met a lady by the name of Tanye Parker. She was very strong minded. She saw that I had begun growing my hair so she offered to braid it; for a fee of course.

Tanya and I lived on the same floor of the apartment complex. She had four children. Two daughters and two boys. The oldest was a girl who lived on her own and the other was around my age and two more that was few years younger. They became pretty fond of me. The boys would come to my apartment often. We were around the same age. They enjoyed my cooking and the saw that I took care of myself and paid my own bills.

I had taken care of most of my court issues and applied for a job at the National Bank of Commerce in downtown Memphis on main street. It was a job as General Ledger Reconciliation Specialist. I had to balance the account of thirteen major branches along the east coast. I was hired under the supervision of Maria Srnka. I had to prepare monthly, weekly and quarterly reports to the department heads of the National Bank of Commerce. The bank was getting ready to merge with another bank and become SunTrust Bank. in the process of working, my hands and knees swelled up causing me to miss work in the weeks of the merger. Even though I was given a raise for balancing the accounts in such short time, I was still fired for job abandonment. I had no money saved up and no one to depend on. I did not pursue legal action against my job for wrongful termination. I went and got a job at a local restaurant as a waiter.

Waiting tables game me much freedom and I could literally be myself and move around. I made money daily and focused on my court cases. While working for Landry's Seafood Restaurant, I met a guy named Micheal Vaughn. He had a daughter named Gabrielle. He was short and very handsome. Very nice in his tone of voice. He offer to assist me with rent if I let him move in with me so he could be closer to work.

I felt like nothing could go wrong because he seemed like a trustworthy person.

Months went by and our friendship became closer. I eventually met his daughter on occasion. I was beginning to feel a sense of friendship.

I got a part-time job at H&R Block again since I had worked for them while I was in the Navy. Micheal had promised that he would pay his share of the rent from his tax returns.

So I began to look forward to it. Work was pretty rewarding, I was good at waiting tables. It was far from aviation and banking. I had a lot of freedom. I got to choose what days I wanted to work. With the money Micheal had promised, I was going to pay up the rent and pay off the remainder of my court cost.

Tax season ended and Micheal began to become more friendly. One night he came home drunk and one thing led to another. It was nothing more than a one night fling. Weeks went by and I began to ask for the money for rent that he had promised. He began to make excuses and got upset. I left and went to work. I returned home and found Micheal laying on the couch. He wasn't expecting me back from work so early as he had been avoiding me in the past weeks. He woke up and seemed upset that I was asking about rent. We began to fight. I went downstairs and got the security guard to call the police.

When the police arrived they asked us if we were a couple. I immediately said "No". I asked them to remove him from my apartment. That was the last I heard from Micheal.

I was missing Robert and all my other friends. It had been well over two years since I had spoken to them. The laws had not changed much. However, the military had decided to allow members to serve and be openly gay.

I decided to leave Memphis and give Texas a chance. I packed up all that I had and move to the state with a friend from work. We decided to get an apartment together. I got a job working at Bank of America. There was nothing sexual between me and this new Micheal. Micheal was openly gay and without me knowing, he decided to get an apartment with a man he had met in Texas. I was left without nothing but my job and an apartment that I could not afford. I became friends with a man and his girlfriend who lived in the apartment who smoke weed constantly. I had not smoked weed since the day I was getting out of the Navy. We smoke daily and I eventually saved enough money to hold on to my apartment. I tried moving my brother out to live with me.

My brother came out to live and made friends with some guys in the neighborhood. For some reason, he was accused of driving a car that was stolen and he made it back to my apartment. I had no choice but to send him back home so he would not go to jail. I moved out of the apartment and moved in with a gay guy named Luther who works at Supercuts.

Luther was openly gay and had a friend named Quincy who I

would often joke around with. They allowed me to stay there for a small fee.

Eventually, I moved out from Luther when I met a man named James. James was very nice. We hit it off very quickly. He offered to pay for an apartment for me so I would not have to see him at Luther's place. Everything seemed to be going okay.

I was settling into my new place and things were going pretty well with James. It seemed as though men were all that GOD would send my way.

I found James very attractive. He was a replacement and reminder of what I was beginning to have with Robert. I had been in my apartment when I received a phone call from a number with a Memphis area code. It was the police. There was another warrant out for my arrest for missing court. They expedited me back to Memphis. I lost my apartment.

I lost track of James and chose to stay in Memphis again with my childhood mentor Mr. Benford and Chris. I lived with them for a few months until I got another apartment in midtown of Memphis, Tennessee.

I got a job working for Isaac Hayes's restaurant. I was a job in the new mall of the Peabody Hotel in downtown Memphis. I enjoyed the music, food and the money that came with work the job. I love the environment. I advanced fast and began training other servers. It paid the bill and got an interest in music. I had the pleasure of meeting Mr. Isaac Hayes himself. I worked the job for about a year until I was accused of stealing. It upset me so much that I quit and quickly got a job on Beale Street working for B.B. King's restaurant. It was even more money than Isaac Hayes's restaurant. I work there for another year.

I was working at B.B. King's and one of my coworkers invited me to the gay pride festival that was happening in Memphis. I agreed to attend. I got all dressed up and caught the attention of a photographer from California who offered me a job as a model. He said all I had to do was come to California and he would take care of the rest. I asked for a transfer to the B.B. Kings that was located at Universal Studios in Hollywood.

It was a big step, but I decided to try out California.

My boss transferred me to the B.B. Kings in Hollywood. I packed up my things and took my dog Dutchess. She was a solid black German Shepard. Very protective.

My mother bought me an Oldsmobile. It was money green in color. I chose to sleep in my car since I could not afford housing and I knew no one in California. It seemed safe. I always parked by a church or under some church light.

I had my probation transferred to California and cleared my community service through the church. I met a white man by the name of Sam whom I became intimate with for a while. We had the love of dogs in common. He had a Siberian husky. It was beautiful grey dog that Dutchess came to get along with. We went camping often and I began to fall in love with nature and the outdoors, I still had no desire to return home. There was really no need for me to return home.

$\mathscr{M}$y time with Sam eventually came to an end and I moved on with Dutchess. My job at B.B. Kings came to an end and my photo session never happened because the photographer wanted sex. I lived in my car with my dog for almost two years selling my poetry out of my car. I got a membership at the gym so I could take showers and got another job waiting table at Gladstones Seafood restaurant in Universal Studios City Walk.

I found an apartment on Lankershim Boulevard and remained to myself. Life seemed peaceful despite its struggles.

It had been five years since I was discharged. I had managed to reconnect with Ross from the Navy. She was in Texas. She was doing pretty good for herself. I made plans to visit during gay pride.

I made the trip to Texas to visit Ross. She lived in a huge apartment in Houston and she worked for the city. She had gotten comfortable with her lifestyle. I was only going to be in town for a few days. It was so good to see her. It was like our friendship had never ended. She wanted to show me around the city and we went to see her mom. Her mom was very nice.

We got ready and made plans to ride down to Galveston, Texas for the gay pride events. Gays had come along way. We still had a long way to go in regards to respect.

We made it to Galveston and found the beach was packed with people from all walks of life. Many people were out with their families. I had never seen so many gay people in my life. If I ever felt a sense of belonging, it was then.

My visit with Ross wasn't long as I had to return to California for an interview with Verizon Wireless. Life was yet still, all work and no play.

California is a beautiful state. So much more to get into than Mississippi. I had no intentions of returning home. It seemed as though my parents fought less if was not under their roof. Besides, I was too old to be living at home.

I got the job at Verizon Wireless. They had great benefits. Dutchess and I got settled into the apartment in North Hollywood. My visit with Ross only made me feel more depressed. I wasn't much of a drinker but I began attending Alcoholics Anonymous meetings to cope with depression.

The job with Verizon paid well for my age. I chose not to get a car because of fear of being pulled over by the police and having legal issues to resurface. I used a bicycle and the caught public transportation as often as possible to get to work.

"If there is a Will, there is a Way".

No matter what, it seemed as though the Spirit of GOD had always been with me. I found pleasure in going to a local junior high school to open mic and spoken word sessions. It was what I needed to express myself and relieve stress. I got the courage to type my poetry books and send them off to be copyrighted. I was always good with words.

I found a couple of places that offered freedom of expression so I could vent. I was walking by a casting agency when I passed an open door. There was a lady sitting inside on the phone booking clients. Her name was Kimberly.

As I sat and waited for her to get off the phone she asked me what was I doing in her neighborhood. I told her that I was on lunch break, just passing time. After exchanging a few words we exchanged numbers and she informed me that she was a casting agent who was looking for people to do audience work. All I had to do was sit in in the audience and get paid. I could do that on my days off from Verizon and Gladstones.

One of my coworkers from Gladstones invited me to go on a camping trip in Eagle Rock. She liked dogs, so I brought Dutchess along.

We got to the campsite and had to walk down a long trail to a location where the water flowed down the mountainside into a pool. We didn't know if snakes were in the water but we took the chance of going for an immediate swim.

Maricella stripped down to her bikini so she could bathe in the sun. I was used to having naked girls around me from my time in college and my encounters with lesbians that Mr. Benford knew. It was Dutchess's first time being in the water. She didn't hesitate to jump into the natural pool.

We pulled out the grill and got ready for dinner. It had been a long time since I had been camping. It felt good to be one with nature. Listening to the water run down the mountainside. We could hear the coyotes in the distance. We spent the night there.

The next morning we packed up the gear and headed back to the city.

Maricella was a beautiful Hispanic female, but I knew that there was nothing that was going to happen sexually between us. It was nothing more than a work relationship. She was becoming more of a sister.

I was still in the training period for Verizon Wireless. Gladstones was a great job but I could no longer leave Dutchess by herself all day without anyone to walk her. She was growing pretty fast. She seemed to love me very much.

Training for Verizon was all the way in Costa Mesa, California. I had met another guy who had car and allowed me to drive it to training class and pick him up everyday. He was very fond of me and happy to help me.

I completed the training for Verizon Wireless. On my job at Gladstones, I had become friends with a guy name Paul. He was so handsome and tall. He was very protective of his personal space. I asked him to help me paint my apartment. It was the only way I could get to spend time with him. He shared an interest in spoken word and open mic. He rapped on the side.

Paul and I became good friends. I would go over to his apartment and spend hours and hours with him. He reminded me of Robert.

He told me that I was talented and should not be in California unless I was trying to do something with myself. He gave me compliments and uplifted me. It was the first time a man had done so.

We spent more and more time together. We were going to the studio and other activities that involved the music industry.

I called and spoke with my mother when I was at Paul's place. I allowed Paul to speak to my mother so I could give her a sense of comfort that I was hanging out with someone who was sane. She could tell that I liked him.

I wasn't long before I had another episode of the bad knees and was in too much pain to work. I went to the local Veterans Affairs hospital. I was then told that I should apply for military benefits. I had only served roughly four years and I felt guilty about asking for help. The hospital said that I was entitled to the benefits so I applied. It seemed as though GOD was blessing me again.

# 12

*Dwight* D. Eisenhower said "The most courageous thing you can do is ask for help". It had been five years since I was discharged from the military. Life had been odd jobs and loosing those jobs because of the pain from injuries that occurred during my military service. It was only the beginning when I applied for benefits with the Veterans Affairs hospital. They wanted to know every single emotional detail of my life; before and after service up until that point. They sent me to Oxnard, California for a medical evaluation. I was diagnosed with PTSD.

I left the medical evaluation feeling more frustrated but relieved. At least everything was on record now and I would possibly receive some assistance from the veteran administration. I knew they could not change the past, but they could assist with a better future.

I decided to do some site seeing so I drove up to Ventura, California. It was only about a fifteen minute drive from Oxnard. Dutchess and I got a hotel by the beach.

Later in the evening I went out for dinner. I left Dutchess in the room. I stopped in at a local bar call the "Goody Bar". I walked into the bar and it was karaoke night. I signed up to sing. It was pretty crowded, so I chose a seat at the bar and ordered with the bartender.

About an hour went by and it was finally my time to sing. I sang a song by Marvin Gaye; "Sexual Healing".

I began singing and everyone started gathering around the stage to dance. It was only a karaoke song, but it felt good to move the crowd with my voice. After singing, I got a round of applause and headed back to my seat. A guy was staring at me and headed over in my direction.

He introduced himself as Rick. He said, "You were awesome". I said, "Thanks for the compliment". He continued by asking what do I do for a living? I said, "I've just been working odd jobs and I'm just in town on military business. Just passing time". He said, "You should look into going into the studio to record some music". I just laughed it off because I had severe stage fright.

Nevertheless, I signed up for more and more songs to sing. Hours had past. Rick and I became good friends and he invited me over to his house for drinks. Rick was a disk jockey and studying accounting in school. He had big dreams. He managed a few bands and had a few connections in Ventura. We exchanged numbers and ideas. I was at his house for a few hours before I returned to my room to walk Dutchess.

I checked out of the hotel and went to meet Rick for lunch before heading back to Los Angeles.

The job at Verizon Wireless was very rewarding. It was the first job I had that supported gay marriage, but I was planning on marriage anytime soon. I honestly had not met anyone that could take my mind off of Robert.

I finished my training and was given a position at the Santa Monica and Wilshire location. It was a fast paced environment. All sorts of people came into the store. I eventually decided to let my job at Gladstones go because of the income at Verizon Wireless.

There is nothing in the world more rewarding than providing for yourself. Sometimes you have good days. Sometimes you have bad days, but you get up every day and repeat the motions. You meet people who make you feel good about yourself and you meet people that make you question you existence. California was like the land of milk and honey. It's a melting pot of all walks of life. It's a place to find yourself.

You have to find a way to laugh at life when you been through a lot and keep it to yourself. No one is going to hold your hand all the time. There will be ups and downs.

My mom was happy that I had moved out of my car and into an apartment. She knew that I was trying to make a living and did not want to return home. Besides, my relationship with my father was not great. I would call home and talk to my mother and occasionally I would try to hold conversation with Charles. We just never formed the father and son bond after all the abuse I had witnessed. My mom felt so strongly about her vows that she chose to stay with him regardless of the verbal abuse.

I was forced to leave their relationship between the two of them. My mother said "A child must stay in a child's place". Even though I always felt as though I was placed in the shoes of an adult.

I felt bad about calling to ask for money so I chose to provide for myself. I felt good about sending money home to my mother to help out because Charles had become ill. Regardless of how Charles had treated me as a child, I still felt a spiritual obligation to give back to my parents. Besides, his treatment could have been worse if I was not for my grandfather always coming to defend my mother. My grandfather knew Charles had a temper.

I could not let past drama in my childhood continue to interfere with how I interacted with people whom had not done me wrong. However, I had to keep my guard up against deception because everyone is not going to treat me like my mother.

I reconnected with Kimberly from the casting agency and went to work on a few television shows doing audience work to pass time. It was easy for the walls to come closing in when you are stuck in the house all day.

Kimberly was always full of energy. She was like a big sister to me. She was fond of dogs, so she would allow me to bring Dutchess along when I visited her at the office. We would sit in her office while she made calls and booked the cast for different shows she was working on. Anytime I was with her, we would have a good time.

Before long, Kimberly was like family. On most of my days off, I would go and hang out with her. She would give me sit in jobs in the audience so I could make extra money and I appreciated it. I was constantly sending money home to help my mother out with the bills. As long as my bills were paid, I was able to help. My mother appreciated every bit of help because my father was now unable to work. His years of drug and alcohol use had caught up with him.

After all that I had witnessed between my parents, I knew that they loved each other. I didn't feel right holding grudges. Judgement was inevitable. They raised me the best that they could. They still were not aware of my molestation, but they were very aware of my mannerism and my sexuality. Even though they did not agree, they did the best thing they could do. They put me in GOD's hands.

I saw that GOD had created all things and I believe that GOD had created all things. Life was yet still, all work and no play. I was waking up at four o'clock to get to work by seven o'clock a.m. I would walk Dutchess early in the morning and leave her in her cage so she would not mess up the apartment. Over time, she learned how to get out of her cage. She was not like any other dog. She quickly became the love of my life.

I remembered getting Dutchess from a cousin of mines in Mississippi. She was a solid black German Shepard. She was very protective. Everywhere I went, there would be Dutchess. I felt guilty about leaving her in the cage, but after disciplining her she learned to use the restroom in her cage and sometimes she would use the flower pot because she would be in the restroom with me in my apartment. We took showers together and slept in the same bed. She was the first female form of anything that I ever loved, other than my mother.

On some days, when I worked long hours, I would allow Paul to look after Dutchess so she would not be alone, Even though she was protective, she found a way to allow others around us.

On one occasion, when I was going through the process of getting my military benefits, I had to be hospitalized for an entire month. I went to PAWS and they assigned me a foster parent for Dutchess. She was a white lady named Jackie. I gave her full instruction on how to handle my dog.

I informed Ms. Jackie to not shake hands in front of Dutchess and if she had company, do not let anyone see Dutchess because she would go in to protection mode, I tried to warn her. Ms. Jackie said that she stopped to get gas in her neighborhood. A friend saw her at the pump and wanted to stop and speak with her about something. She had just picked Dutchess up to begin temporary foster care while I was in the hospital. She said she thought Dutchess was going to break through her window to attack her friend because she had never seen a dog act so protective. She had to end the conversation quickly with her friend because it was making a big scene at the pump. She said that in that moment, she wanted a dog like Dutchess. She made it through the entire month and said she never slept so well.

I got Dutchess back and she was so happy to see me. I was happy that Ms. Jackie had taken good care of her. I thanked her and that was the last time I saw her.

The time in the hospital was more stressful than I thought, I was in a place full of veterans who had served and had similar experiences before and after our military service. However, it felt good that someone was listening, That was honestly all that I wanted. Living a life of ridicule and discrimination was catching up to my own health. After the hospital ran all their tests, I found out that my immune system had suffered from stress. Holding in emotions and unexpressed feelings was taking toll. It was time to let go of childish things.

I went to into isolation and only focused on work. It was weekly meetings with my psychologist about every single event that was happening and events that had already happened. It was embarrassing, and at often times painful to confess that I had experienced so much. When I asked my doctors if they had experienced what I had experienced, most of the time they said "no". The most frustrating thing they would say was "You are rambling". I thought how would they understand what I was going through.

So, I asked for a psychologist that was openly gay even though I felt as though I was living a "closeted life".

Even though I was receiving medical help, my family and other that knew me thought I was trying to run a "con" on the government. I could not fake x-rays, cat scans and MRIs. Life at sea had taken its toll on my body. The stresses of daily interaction had taken toll on my peace of mind. The only sanity I had was found in the knowledge of GOD's creation.

Traveling with the military had opened my eyes to people of the world and the foundation I received from my childhood only made it harder to understand rights and wrong, fairness and privilege, hard work and laziness. There was no closing my eyes nor my heart on life.

## 13

The love of money is the root of all evil. GOD works fast when you put work into your prayers. It took only six months. After verifying my injuries and events that occurred during my military service, the Veterans Affairs office approved my benefits. Even though it was blessing, it quickly began to be a burden.

I continued working at Verizon Wireless because of the fear of getting comfortable with receiving benefits and the government changes its mind. After about two years on the job, my eyes were getting bad. I was advised to get a corneal transplant. They said that my immune system was too low for immediate surgery and I was not a candidate for corrective surgery. I was told that I needed to rest. Rest was not in my being. I was simply used to working hard.

I called my grandfather and spoke with him about the time we watched him have eye surgery and I had to administer eye drops to his eye for a year. The recovery time was too long for me to spare. Luckily I had been approved for benefits through the military.

I had great benefits at Verizon Wireless, but even better benefits through the Veterans Affairs hospital.

I had a cousin who I grew up with who wanted to experience California, so I invited him to come live with me while I rested for surgery. I thought it would be good to have family nearby. I let him bring his girlfriend who was pregnant as well.

I drove to Mississippi for my birthday and brought my cousin and his girlfriend back out to live with Dutchess and I. I was happy having them out with me in California, but a house of grown people can quickly gather tension if there is not honest communication.

They say, "The road to Hell is paved with good intentions".

In the middle of going to meetings with my psychologist, I found myself trying to be a mentor and a counselor to my cousin. But, what could I honestly tell a grown man. I quickly learn that the relationship between my cousin and his girlfriend was like the relationship between my parents. I felt like it was causing stress to the baby so I did things to try to minimize stress. They weren't working and were not looking for jobs and I wasn't asking them to because it wasn't part of the communication. With the money I was receiving, plus that from my job, I planned to pay all the bills. I was always at work so, most of the time they had the apartment to themselves.

A few months had passed and my cousin's girlfriend was getting closer to having the baby. I was so excited. I felt like I had been very supportive, but I knew she wanted to have the baby in Mississippi.

I took Rick's advice and went and bought the music equipment for a personal studio and while I was at work, my cousin work on his music. I hardly had time to work on my own. I felt like it would minimize the arguments and there would be less stress on his girlfriend and the baby. Everyone on my job knew I had my cousin and his girlfriend living with me. To my surprise, everyone wondered why I would let two straight people live with me. Even more, my cousin and his girlfriend were an interracial couple.

I got a phone call in the middle of the night. It was my cousin's brother. He felt like he was in trouble with the law. He said he didn't have any money and want to get out of the south. I already had his brother and his girlfriend living with me until the baby was due, but I agreed to let him come to California as well. So, I purchased a Greyhound bus ticket. One way.

My cousin and his brother were like oil and water; sibling rivalry when they were younger. Regardless, I was willing to give living under one roof a try. Their mother, my aunt, said that they looked up to me and I knew that they did. However, the road to maturity would be long.

All four of us, and the baby to come, we settled into the apartment. Right away, the brother enrolled in school. I felt like it was a step towards maturity and growth. Nevertheless, immaturity was still present. The brother who had the girlfriend was becoming jealous of his younger brother's progress and thought that I was showing favoritism, since I was assisting with paying for school and buying clothes. It was almost like I went into parent mode, but they remained in cousin mode.

I continued to say to my cousins, "This is not Mississippi, this is California. The opportunities are here".

My cousin's girlfriend was getting bigger and bigger. The baby was not too far away. I asked my cousin and his girlfriend to simply keep the house clean since I was paying all the bills. I figured that was fair. I was mostly concerned about the baby.

After about another month, tension between the brothers was rising. The older cousin was taking his frustration out on his girlfriend and the younger cousin was too busy to listen. With me being at work all the time, I barely knew what any argument was about. Regardless, it was time to send the older brother and his girlfriend home so she could have the baby. We were sitting in the apartment. My cousins began to argue about who was doing more around the apartment and why the girlfriend never had to do much. The argument cause the older brother to grab the biggest knife in the kitchen and go charging at his younger brother. I got up just in time to grab his wrist before stabbing his brother in the chest. I got cut on my hand in the process. Immediately, I called the girlfriend's grandmother and let her know that I was sending them home that night.

They older cousin was upset with me, but regardless of the argument, I didn't know any woman that kept a baby in their womb over nine months, so I sent them home so she could have her baby around family. My cousin never forgave me. It was his responsibility to go home with her and the time had come.

The younger cousin and I were trying to work out our living arrangement and I was trying to show him responsibility and accountancy for his life. I was trying to erase the stereotype. Besides he was on the run from what he had done to get in trouble with the police.

Judgement is a part of life. Regardless of if a person is receiving judgement or giving judgement, we cannot help what someone thinks of us. The past is the past, however, it will follow you and keep you in a crossroads with how you see yourself.

I was cleaning up the apartment and found a letter that my cousin's girlfriend had written to her grandmother. I had no choice but to read it. When reading the letter I discovered that the girlfriend was very unappreciative. She was saying very negative things in the letter regarding my sexuality. So I called the grandmother and read the letter to her. It was best I sent them home.

The younger cousin and I would have discussions on what they wanted to do to make things better in the apartment since he was going to be living with me until he got on his feet. I wanted him to keep busy and stay out of trouble since he was on the run from the police. The plan was that he would get his probation transferred to California.

# 14

You can and only be yourself. No matter how many smiles you put on someone's face, money can't buy love. In an effort to help, some actions can be misunderstood. In other words, if you can't help someone, don't hinder them.

The younger cousin was getting settled into living in California. He was making new friends. I was planning to take off work in order to rest and build up my immune system for the corneal transplant. It was just Dutchess, my cousin, and I living in the apartment. I didn't know how it would be living with my cousin. We both had different belief systems. We had different ways of life. For the most part, he was heterosexual and I was homosexual. But, we loved each other.

When you understand the nature of a person you begin to expect the goods and the bad that come along with having them in your space.

It was now 2006. I was twenty-seven years old. My friends were now wondering why I would move people into my house who did not approve of my lifestyle. The thought of having someone live with you who felt that you were going to burn in hell was unbearable to them. I would constantly say, "I'll do just about anything for family".

My cousin was doing well in school and I was still at work. The money was good and I was able to assist with paying for his school. Things seemed to be going fine.

I was only about four years older than my cousin, but there I was being a mentor and feeling like a father figure. I knew it was not my responsibility to keep him out of trouble, but I felt like the more questions I asked… the more frustration would arise, so I remained focused on work and healing.

I was at work doing a double shift. My cousin thought that I was at home. He had lost the spare key and could not get into the apartment. In his impatience, he decided to break into the apartment by kicking the door open. In doing so, the doorknob put a hole in the wall of my apartment. Since I was not supposed to have anyone living with me, I decided to repair the hole as best as I could and move out of the apartment. I was too embarrassed to mention the incident to the apartment manager. I quickly found a two bedroom apartment in Hollywood on Mansfield Ave.

In the middle of dealing with my cousin, I was having my own identity crisis. I was being forced to use the name that I was born with instead of the name my mother married. The government said that my birth certificate did not match my social security card. My birth name was Porter and my mother had married Moore. When I was younger, I said that my name would come back to haunt me. It was as if everything I had worked for was about to be erased from existence.

It was time to get my license renewed. I went to the Department of Motor Vehicles with my birth certificate and the social security card that I had at the time. The clerk said that I could not get my license renewed unless the names matched. I was forced to contact the Department of Vital Records in Mississippi.

I contacted the Department of Vital Records and the receptionist asked for my name. I stated the name that I was going by at the time. I said, "Jeffrey SHILOYNE Moore. She said, "There is no one on record with that name." So I gave her the name that I was born with. I said, "Try Jeffrey Shiloyne Porter". She quickly asked, "Why do you have two names". I began explaining my life story. The receptionist said, "I am sorry that happened to you".

The receptionist said, "I can only send the birth certificate with the name Jeffrey Shiloyne Porter". I said, "Okay".

It was like GOD was sending me down some path. I remembered being in second grade and being forced to change my name because Charles wanted everyone in the house to have the same name. I didn't think it would cause so many problems at the age of twenty-seven.

She said, "Your birth certificate will be there in three to five days Mr. Porter". I felt relieved to be using my original name again. But that was only the beginning.

I called my mother and informed her that I had to go by my original name. At first she was upset, but then she understood that law was the law. I was the one who had to live with the consequences.

My birth certificate arrived and I went to the Social Security Administration and asked for a new card for the name ending in Porter. The clerk typed in my name and found that I already had a number that existed. The only identification I had had the name ending in Moore. The clerk asked for my identification and when she looked at it she walked back got the supervisor. They thought that I was trying to commit fraud or that I was married because I had two last names. She did not bother to look up my other social and she proceeded to look in to the name ending in Porter. She said I was twelve years old when my parents changed my name. She handed me back my identification after I found myself once again explaining my life story. She said my original social security card would arrive in five to seven business days.

I left the Social Security Administration talking to GOD. A part of me was afraid of losing everything I had worked on in regards to my identity. Another part of me was relieved that I could now live using the name I was born with. It was almost as if I was given the chance to start over in life.

I remained focused on helping my cousin and taking care of the bills. My friends thought that I was being distant and taking care of business. They felt as though I was being used. I constantly stated that I'd do anything for family. Besides, he was getting on his feet.

There was nothing more important to me than my reputation with family. Even though they mostly knew of my sexuality, I never brought my lifestyle up around them. It was like I was living two or more lives. I went deeper and deeper into a state of depression and only focused on making family happy.

It was quick to discover that my cousin and I had very different ways of living. The two bedroom apartment gave us space from each other. I was trying to get comfortable with using my name on a regular basis. I went to the federal building on Wilshire Boulevard and informed the government of what had taken place at the Social Security Administration. I was trying to keep my identity in order.

To get away from stress I took camping trip. I figured nature would give me the healing that I needed. I didn't want to force my beliefs on my cousin and I was not about to allow judgement to rule love. Up until then, I had been really close to all of my family. I had swept most of my childhood emotions under some imaginary carpet and attempt the traditional, somewhat normal way of life. I knew I had been through a lot and witnessed a lot. Trying to keep secrets that questioned my identity and matters of unconditional love often caused times of loneliness and stress but I knew GOD was with me. Even though I could not see GOD, I felt the presence in GOD's lessons. Just like my mother, I was trying to honor the marriage, but the law had begun to rectify the past. In rectifying the past, it was causing me to stand up and speak up for myself. I learned resilience and patience, but I also learned humility and compassion. Honestly, all I had was myself to depend on.

## 15

*B*esides work, all I had done was remain to myself. In my acceptance of reality, I could look around and see that GOD had made a beautiful world. In all of the Universe's creation, our planet is the most unique because of the life that lives on it. For me, life had been nomadic, obedient, respectful, beautiful, full of lessons from my childhood, many long conversations with GOD, many goods and many evils. I had to learn how to get over moments where I bit my tongue, gritted my teeth, or simply took the "higher road" and walked away. I had cried myself to sleep because of judgement and ridicule. I had simply given up on the thought of love and replaced it with loyalty if I would come in human form.

In 1990 I was forced to change my last name because of marriage. I guess traditionally, in a marriage, everyone would have the same last name. Maybe it was done so just to make things in the household look good. But, what does that have to do respect, honor, love and loyalty. By May of 2007, I was being forced to change my name back

to its original name because of the Patriot Act. There was a clause in
the Act that stated that all documents regarding identity must match.
Since you can't change the name on the birth certificate, the social
security card must match the birth certificate.

All I had was my identity, my entire family called me Shaun. As
far as my legal name, it was cause more and more stress in the family.
Some who didn't know the past or the truth, thought I was rebelling.
To myself, twenty-eight years of age was not the time to rebel. I had
learned to adjust to my name change as a child and now as an adult,
I understood the law. There was clearly no rebellion.

I decided to take a camping trip and ride up the coast line. I love to
look at the mountains and ride the hills and curves along the Oceanside.
I made friends with a man named John who was a photographer. We
were going up to San Francisco. I had never been. We were going to
take some pictures and camp out in the mountains. I felt that I could
give my cousin some space and I could get some relaxation. The new
apartment was not working out and I just want to get away.

Someone once told me, "You can always make knew friends". I
had decided to break the lease and move into my car. I had lived in
my car for two years before and sold poetry books out of my car when
I first moved to California. My cousin had made new friends and I
was getting uncomfortable with whom he was hanging out with. I
figured he would be okay if he was making new friends.

I began packing up all the furniture and simply left a couch on
the balcony. It had not been long since I moved into the apartment
so I didn't have much to move out. John was living in his car while
visiting from San Francisco so I offered for him to sleep on the couch.
John was a white man, possibly Jewish or Greek. My cousin thought
that John and I had some sexual relationship going on. We were just
merely platonic friends.

I packed up everything in the apartment. I was walking to the storage facility with a load of belongings. The storage facility was on Santa Monica near Mansfield, so it was walking distance. I was questioning my existence. I was wondering why I was going through so much stress. I was contemplating suicide. I thought, if I didn't succeed at trying to kill myself, I may be left in some mental state or become physically disabled.

I had a bottle of medicine that I had been prescribed from my psychiatrist. I thought, no one would really miss me or care if I killed myself because of my sexuality. I thought that if I did not succeed and I was left in the state of mind that I was in, then GOD must have given me life for a reason that I did not yet know. I waited until I was home alone and I took the bottle of mirtazipine with a coke. I placed my life in GOD's hands.

The next morning I woke up and realized that pills were not effective. I didn't know if I had upset GOD with my attempt at taking my life, but I knew I was not brave enough to attempt it again.

I got my bible out and I began reading. I began asking if I had been here before. Had I lived in any other form before in time? Why did GOD not allow me to die?

I decided to go for a walk and take more things to the storage unit. My cousin was returning home. He saw that I had cleaned out the apartment and was ready to move out. I grabbed my bible and was walking and reading. I made it to the corner of Fountain and Mansfield. I was thinking about changing my mind and taking everything out of storage and putting it back into the apartment. A part of me felt as though I was abandoning my cousin and the other part of me felt as though my cousin was a grown man and we were two completely different individuals. So I asked GOD to give me a sign. Specifically, I asked for the "Almighty Creator" to place marks on my two peace fingers so that I would know that my life was valuable. I took a few more steps and came across the scripture John 1:27. It's a Scripture pertaining to untying the sandals of Jesus. In that moment, two marks appeared on my hand. The marks appeared on the knuckles of my peace fingers on my right hand. I began to cry and I licked the blood from my hand. I began to cry and quickly returned to my apartment.

I rushed into the door saying that something had bit me. It was the most spiritual moment I had ever experienced. I thought about all that had been created up until now and asked "why me?" After everything that I had experienced, why was the Universe or GOD giving me this sign.

My cousin saw my hand bleeding and thought that I had been in a fight. I kept insisting that it was GOD and my prayer had been answered. But my cousin failed to accept that it had happened. I had no witness. The most unusual thing to happen was that the radio would become static. White noise. Most people say that's from the spirit world. I had came across a new reality and I did not know anyone in existence that had experienced stigmata.

I looked on the internet and the country of India was discussing gender and sexual identity. They were talking about gender and sexual behavior. Heterosexual, homosexual, and bisexual behavior had been in existence so millennia. Gay rights and marriage were on the table to become law and the song "Same Love" was just coming out. The astronaut's wife had been shot in the head and Jim Carey became the new host of The Price Is Right. The white noise was everywhere in the apartment. I was living in apartment 307. I knew words were powerful and some people studied numerology. Scientology was the new religion. The were many powerful leader in the religious community speaking on the radio and many radio stations were complaining and amazed about the interference that came from the white noise. I went to the corner of the apartment and balled up and waited for my camping trip.

John came and was done shooting the photography. My hand had long stopped bleeding but I was wearing a black glove to cover up the marks and minimize questions. I cried constantly and thought that many people were upset and angry because of the events that were happening on the internet. I wondered who I truly was. I didn't say much to John and he could feel the tension in the house. He questioned the "white noise" that was on the radio so I turn off the radio. I didn't want to make him any more uncomfortable than I was. I was overwhelmed with sadness and gratitude that something had listened to my prayers. My understanding of life had been changed in an instance and I had no way to explain it. I knew that no one would believe me and the only thing I had to prove that anything had happened were the marks on my hand. But the marks were beginning to heal and soon it would just be a part of life that happened.

I was ready to take the camping trip but my cousin thought that I was having a nervous breakdown.

I was not going to go running down the street screaming at anything invisible. I opened my laptop and accidentally stumble across zoroastrianism. It's a religion that spoke of a prophet who was contacted by the spirit of good and evil. My laptop just accidentally led me to it. I had been called a many things in life, but I felt far from a prophet. I did however want to learn more about what had happened to me in regards to the marks on my hand.

Eventually the white noise in the house became unbearable. I called the ambulance because of the noises that I was constantly hearing with in the apartment. It honestly felt as though some spiritual or paranormal activity was taking place.

The ambulance arrived and took me to the Veterans Affairs Hospital in West Los Angeles. They were only going to call me crazy if I mentioned anything about the marks and how they appeared on my hand. A part of me felt as though some people knew, but I knew I had no one walking with me when the marks appeared. For me, it was as if GOD or my guardian angel was answering my prayers. I had just attempted suicide the night before and immediately the next day I was receiving the most spiritual sign that I could have imagined.

I had read about verses and scripture where humans could not handle the sight of GOD and that coming too close into contact with GOD would cause death. But that was information based on the Bible and written thousands of years ago. There were so many good books to read. Some of those books were older than the Bible and they had their own stories of miracles and testimonies from psychics, religious leaders and spiritual advisors throughout history. Yet, I was living in now 2007 and experiencing stigmata in a minor form. The incident happened on July 7, 2007. 777. Lucky numbers. So I felt blessed. But I was still fearful of what I could do and what others thought about the unknown.

Regardless of my previous reality. I had embarked on a different path in life. I knew that I didn't want to leave anyone behind. As far as I knew, I was still human. Nothing had changed. I was feeling a little bit more comfortable with my existence, but I was still lonely.

I sat in the hospital room with the marks on my hand. No one noticed. Only I knew what had happened. I was laying on my bed when I came out of my sleep. The nurse said that I had been asleep for three days. The hospital had been monitoring me. All I noticed was the flickering lights and I had a very bad headache. I remembered being drained of energy.

After a few hours, my cousin arrived at the hospital worried about my mental health. I was ready to get home and get back to my dog Dutchess, but the hospital wanted to run more test. They were all concerned about my mental health. They didn't know what I had experienced and for some reason I felt as though it would be hard to explain. So I went along with the medical procedures and ate the food and talked to my cousin.

I let him know that I was moving out of the apartment because of maintenance. I said that because I did not want him to know about the stress of living with him. I asked the nurse if I could go outside for smoke and she said I could. I wanted to smoke a blunt. I wanted some marijuana so I could relax,

My cousin and I went to his car and smoked, I let him know of my intentions to live in my car until I found another place to live. I needed time to myself.

# 16

*ife will hit you hard if you've never been through anything. If you feel you were never truly loved, life can be very depressing. Especially, when you live to please everyone but yourself. Up until now, I realized that money could not buy me love. If a person had not experienced what I had experienced, all they could say was that they were sorry that I had experienced those things. I found myself telling people that they did not have to apologize for what others had done to me. Sometimes I would find people doing things that people had done just because they knew I would forgive them. Forgiveness was something I had mad a habit of.

I got out of the hospital after a few days. I was on a medical hold called a 5150. I made it back to the apartment and called John to let him know that he could come by for the night. I had a few days before I would be completely out of the apartment. There was still confusion and tension in the apartment between my cousin and I so we packed for the camping trip. I needed to get away for the fresh air.

We drove up to San Francisco where John lived. The coastline from Los Angeles include Malibu, Ventura, Santa Barbara and many other cities. We went to a district called "Hate Ashbury". It was a major tourist attraction. It had been a while since I had been anywhere to relax. We walked around for a few hours before we went to John's house to meet his girlfriend, Shelly, who lived in the Berkeley area.

Shelly was a blonde lady with hair down to her waist. She was more of a hippie type woman. Very free. She welcomed me into her place and told me which room I would be sleeping in. Once I saw that she had a patio, I asked her if I could sleep on the patio because the weather was so nice. She asked why and I said because we were going to be outside camping anyway, She agreed.

All I could think about were the marks on my hand. I really hadn't spoken much to John, but he already knew I wasn't much of a talker. I just enjoyed his energy and the conversations he would initiate. It gave me time to listen to the voice within. Besides, John had been away from Shelly for a few days and they were enjoying each other's time. I sat on the patio and looked at the stars for a while before dozing off.

The next morning John and I went up to Lake Tahoe to begin our camping trip. He, Dutchess and I found a spot along the river. Dutchess jumped out the car and ran straight for the water. It was a beautiful site down in the valley of the Rocky Mountains. We unpacked the car and set up the campsite.

John let me know that his dad was in the CIA. I let him know that I was once in the Navy. We talked about many things for hours and hours. We had food in the cooler so fired up the grill once the sun went down and made ourselves comfortable.

The next morning we woke up decided to go further up the river to a different camping site. We had packed everything in the car and began driving up the road. I realized that Dutchess was not in the car. We had left her. I looked out the window in the mirror and saw that she was running behind the car. Luckily, we had not begun to pick up speed before I looked back. We pulled over and let her in the car and just laughed to ourselves at the moment. Dutchess was glad to be back in the car. She was licking on both of us. We were amazed that she kept up with the car.

We made it to the next camping site. It was more up by the lake. We only had one more day before I had to be back at work and my vacation was going to be over. All that I had ever known was work. I had never taken a real vacation up until now. I was always so used to working. Having a dog gave me a sense of responsibility, but having a friend gave me a sense of humanity. My friendship had always consisted of family. I had gone to school with people of different races and served in the military with multiple races and genders but I had never been around a man for a long period of time and it wasn't sexual. John was open-minded to my sexuality and was not judgmental, so it felt more human and more natural to be around him. Dutchess liked his energy as well.

We spent the rest of the day there and was going to drive home to Los Angeles in the night time when traffic had died down. We were about to pack up but heard that there was an 18-wheeler accident on the bridge that crossed over the bay. It was a blessing that we did not leave for home when we planned to because we could have been a part of the accident.

Once the accident was cleared, we headed back to Los Angeles. My mom called to check and see if I was alright as usual. She had heard and seen the accident on the news. I told her that I was fine. I let her speak to John for a brief moment because she overheard him

By Grace and Grace Alone

talking to me in the car. She always wanted to know what I was doing and who I was doing it with if she had the chance.

Lake Tahoe and the mountains were what I needed to see. It's nice to read and see things in books or on television, but there is nothing like the real life experience. My time with John ended and I was back at home in the presence of white noise and everything that I could come through. In nature, when on the camping trip, there was no technology to interfere with; no radio to listen to and no television. There was just nature. But, back in the apartment and in the car the radio would go static. Sometimes it would turn off. In all of my 28 years of life the only time I knew of interference inside of a car was if the tires were bad or the antenna was damaged. This, to me, was a truly spiritual or paranormal experience. The marks on my hand were turning to a scalp and healing. I was still wearing a glove, but it looked as though I was making a fashion statement. I still didn't have anyone to talk to that I felt safe speaking with about the marks. Mainly because I didn't have a witness and I did not want to go through the judgement of someone perceiving it to be evil.

I knew that I was not evil, but like I said, "There was no one in existence that had gone through stigmata or had their prayers answered in a way that mine were".

I was having visions of the crucifixion. Then *Time Magazine* had a cartoon illustration in their magazine with Hilary Clinton and Mother Teresa at the crucifixion. It was a bit of humor in the magazine, but for me it was a sign or a sort of bad timing. Even for me I knew that what I wanted to discuss sounded crazy. I had gone to GOD in prayer, but the Universe stepped in and I was left with the question of "What or Who came first? God or the Universe?"

Up until now I had been living as a believer of an Almighty God with the knowledge that there were actually, many gods that served under one GOD. However, if there was nothing in existence, what initiated Creation? Did one Creator answer my prayers? If the Creator did answer my prayers or sent/allowed some angel to answer my prayers, then what ability or connection to GOD did I truly possess? What favor did I truly have as a gay man. Within the population of our planet, why was I chosen?

I thought about the beginning of time. Ahura Mazda. Why did I accidentally stumble across some Iranian religion. I did not know my true bloodline. I could only claim positive energy. Most importantly, I wanted to know if whomever or whatever answered my prayers was still listening. How long had IT/GOD been listening. I still had no one to trust. I feared that the diagnosis that I received from the Veterans Affairs Hospital would interfere with someone believing me. I definitely did not want to be laughed at or ridiculed. I certainly was not looking for followers or anyone to preach to. If my words were powerful, I only wanted to use this new gift of contacting the spirit world... for good and good only.

I took my dog to the dog park on Mullholland Drive. She was so protective that she would not play with any of the other dogs. She only wanted to sit beside me or play with me. She was really a uniquely loyal dog.

I was sitting on the bench at the dog park reading *One Day My Soul Just Opened Up by* Iyanla Vanzant. I had read the book several times before. Mainly because it was based on 40 days and 40 nights of meditation. I deeply felt as though the spirit world was still listening. I still had a deep belief in reincarnation and the Afterlife. I felt as though I was deeply in tune with nature.

All of a sudden the dog park got very quiet and the wind began to blow. I saw the little dust tornados and the leaves spiraling. The dogs were not barking and it seemed as though mostly every one was watching Dutchess and I. I continued to read and off in the distance I saw a woman. She was a dark complexion and full figured. She stood there with her hands behind her back. We had been at the dog park well over an hour and I did not see her walk through the gate. It was as if she appeared out of no where. I remained calm because maybe I just did not see her come through the entrance. I thought to myself why is she standing there and facing my direction as if she is looking at me, but I continued to read and focus on Dutchess and I. A few moment passed and it was as if the lady had disappeared.

I was in amazement because the lady reminded me of my grandmother who had passed in 1985.

After about an hour, Dutchess and I went home. I called Rick and asked him to come pick me up. I wanted to get away before I returned to work. I went to Rick's house and the white noise or the spirit world was very present. On the way to his house my hand began to bleed again. I asked for a napkin. Rick said to look in his glove compartment box. I grabbed the napkin and wiped the blood off my hand. I threw the napkin out the window. I said to Rick that he was my Spiritual brother. It was overwhelming for Rick because as soon as I walked through his door the lights flickered and his radio became static. The white line appeared on his television. We both acted as if we didn't notice it.

I knew Rick was in my life for a reason. I was definitely on a spiritual path. I began to notice that if I kept my mind calm, the white noise and the static would not be as bad. He had roommates that already believed in the spirit world and they began to notice what was going on the with the equipment and appliances in Rick's house. Regardless of everything that I felt, I felt the presence of all of our ancestors. Whatever reason we were in each other space, I felt calm and happiness.

*Shiloyne*

Growing up, I learned about different races and cultures. I heard about witchcraft and spirituality. We had teachings of racism and prejudice. There we were, all of different races and nationalities and beliefs. The energy felt good. I felt the presence of my grandmother Rosie. I even smelled roses and there were no roses present. The mark on my hand was noticeable and Ricks roommates asked about it and they knew it was not normal. They asked about my middle name and the pronunciation of it. I told them that it was Hebrew and Indian. I told them that my grandmother on my mother's side was Cherokee Indian. I said "I am a mixture of many things".

Rick offered me his bed to sleep in but I chose to sleep on the couch because of Dutchess.

I had thrown a watch away that I was wearing. It was after midnight and everyone was asleep. I woke up with the covers over my face. I thought I was having a dream. The room honestly looked like constellations were forming. I literally saw stars. I did not choose to wake anyone up or panic because I was already experiencing the unexplainable. If I never had a reason to believe in wormholes or spirit world or any type of paranormal contact, I had a reason to now. Out of thin air, two watches appeared. One watch had a leather band and the other watch was identical to the watch I threw away. I chose the watch that I threw away. I thought maybe the Universe was playing with me. Maybe even GOD was playing with me. I knew my faith was strong. I began to cry. It had been a long time since I had received anything meaningful. I heard the voices of my ancestors. I head a voice that seem to be a woman telling me it was okay to choose and it was the universe helping and blessing me. I placed the watch with the leather band back into the void and cried myself to sleep.

A few hours passed and I visibly saw ghost or apparitions walking through Rick's house. I still remained call because they were walking upstairs to Rick's room but I did not see anyone waking up in fear. The ghosts seem harmless. It hadn't been long since we had attended Rick's grandmother's funeral. I actually believed that I was meant to see them. I chose not to wake anyone up and frighten them because I didn't believe they would see what I was seeing.

Rick heard me walking on the stairs and came out and asked what I was doing. I simply said that I was looking for the restroom. He said if I wanted I could sleep in his room once again. I decided to take his offer.

I slept in Rick's bed and woke up with two blood spots on his pillow. My hand had started bleeding in my sleep. I had an awful headache. Rick said that he had to be somewhere so he could not drive me back to Los Angeles immediately. He said if I wanted to get back soon I could catch the train and he would bring Dutchess later in the day. I thought I would be okay to catch the train and trust Rick with Dutchess. Rick did not bother to mention the blood on his pillow. The only thing I could do was be honest if he did ask.

## 17

ick dropped me off at the train station. I sat there for a minute and noticed a bird that sat on the wire. I believed that the Spirit World communicated in all forms and ways. The experience the previous night at Rick's house only made me more interested in who I was coming and what was I going to be asked to leave behind. I had so many thoughts running through my mind but all I could say to myself was "After all this time, I am the one that GOD wishes to communicate through". But if I was right, then what was this new path that I was on? Why had the watch returned to me? I thought about the beginning of time. I thought about my mother. I mostly thought about my family and my bloodline. I wondered were there other whom had experienced what I went through.

Rick drove away and I had sat there for about 30 minutes. It was as if the train was late for a reason. I don't know what came over me but I began to get completely naked. I was not embarrassed and I it was as if I was being controlled or asked by the spirit world to do so.

After about 10 minutes of sitting there at the train station completely naked, the police arrived and questioned me. Without question I hand them all my identification and began to put my clothes back on. My mind was completely clear and I was aware of what I had done, but the police didn't hesitate to arrest me and take me to a psychiatric hospital in Ventura. The police were more concerned about why I had two last names. I immediately said there is nothing illegal about that. We arrived at the mental health facility and I was checked in.

Every day seem cloudy while I was in the hospital, I remember the nurse rubbing the marks on my hand and constantly asking me what had happened. I said, "You would not believe me if I told you.

After about 5 days I was let go from the 5150 mental health hold. In the hospital, all you have to do is remain quiet and not speak to anyone and eventually they will release you. I called Rick and he was amazed that I was still in Ventura and he was not aware that I had been in the hospital. He came to pick me up from the hospital. I simply remained quiet. I only asked how Dutchess was.

We stopped by his house to pick up Dutchess and head back to Los Angeles. We made it a little past Oxnard California and in a distance I saw a strike of lightning. I asked Rick if he saw that. He said that he did. We continued driving and down the road there was a huge fire. The announcer on the radio was trying to say that the wire was possibly started by someone leaving a fire unattended in the woods. The white noise and static was on the radio in the car. We made it through the fire and they said the fire was getting close to Los Angeles. Rick dropped Dutchess and I off at my apartment and he returned to Ventura. I got to my apartment and my cousin had already moved out so I finished taking things to storage and moved into my car.

The next few weeks it was just Dutchess and I. I began to have a negative feeling about the food I was eating as if I was attached to the life that once flow through the body of what I was eating. I noticed everything around me. I felt guilty about not holding on to the apartment by facing and accepting reality, I knew it was time to move from the racism and the discrimination that seem to flow through the building. I chose the wilderness… so to speak.

I didn't want to return to home to Mississippi because I did not want to overwhelm my family with the spiritual things that were happening but I knew I needed a witness. I needed someone to verify what I was going through. I still had to go back to work.

Many people in California lived in their cars and kept stable jobs. I was still not comfortable with depending on my military benefits as my only income, but I had to find balance with what was now happening in my life.

I figure that Dutchess and I would be okay living in my car and she was a very quiet dog as long as no one disturbed her. At night I live in the hotels for gays and sometime the normal hotels where pets were allow, I worked during the day. I had gotten new contact lenses and opted out on the surgery because there was not a guaranteed recovery. My contact lenses gave me 20/10 vision. Instantly I could see and notice things that I never paid attention to.

I notice everything. I ended up meeting a man whose name I've forgotten. He was everything I desired at this moment in my life. He invited me to a boxing match. I told him that I did not believe in fighting and that if I went to the fight with him he might witness something weird. He looked at my hand and asked what had happened to it. I told him everything and he said "You are a Spiritual Warrior". I said, "I only fight the Devil".

We continued to talk and eventually became intimate. I spent the night at his house and it was the best moments I had ever had. The next morning he cooked me breakfast and we spoke as if we had been in love for centuries. Even though I notice the white noise and he did as well, we figure it was meant to be.

We got ready to go to the boxing match. He, Dutchess and I went to the match together. We arrive at the entrance and while purchasing the tickets to enter, a 20 dollar bill was on the ground next to me. I picked it up, but instead of putting it in my pocket I handed it to the person selling tickets. I noticed the sun come from behind the clouds. We took a few steps and He asked me, "Why didn't you keep that 20?" I said that it wasn't mines. He smiled, we continued to the concession stand and he purchased two beers. He asked, "Aren't you from Louisiana?" I said, "No, but my grandmother was". He said, "So you know about voodoo?" I laughed and said "I don't practice it but I believe in a lot of things". He was very open minded. I notice the sun go behind the clouds and we walked to our seats. We sat down and all of a sudden two black birds began hovering over our section. The speakers in the arena began to sound as if they had noise interference, but I didn't say anything. I was already expecting it by now. It had been happening for months. Next to us there was guy who was staring at me with an angry look as if the birds were there because of me. I tried to ignore him. I slowly sipped my beer. My new love interest slowly sipped his. The birds were still hovering. Out of nowhere the clouds made the day very dark as if it was about to storm or something very powerful present. There was no one standing at the microphone to speak but a voice made a comment that I could have sworn was directed to me, The was a bright light in the parking lot around the arena and the crowd was paying more attention to the Light and the Darkness and the mysterious voice that spoke over the speakers. My date was looking at his tickets and looking at me. The guy sitting next to us was upset that we were sitting next to him. We missed the entire fight and I don't remember the fight ever occurring. The voice stopped, the birds flew away, the sun reappeared and the fight if it ever happened was over. We exited the arena. In the parking lot, the guy who was sitting next to us yelled at me "You fucking Faggot…Do you want HIM to come back". I remained quiet and my date insisted that I keep walking. He said he could see fire in my eyes.

We made it to the car in the parking lot and I began to cry. My hand began to bleed again and he said "You are Rasta". I cried and cried and he kissed my hand. I told him that we could not be together because I was going through something that I did not believe he would understand. I cried all the way to his house. We both heard voices and he asked me why was I letting him go. Even the voices were in approval of us being together. I left.

# 18

*felt* as though I gave up on the love of my life. Once again I chose family over love. I really did not know what was in store for my future and if it was going to be a life of pain, I didn't want to bring anyone into it suffer. I didn't know if I was able to cause things to happen at will. I was honestly unsure of how GOD was going to be presented to me.

I lost track of where he lived just to keep him safe.

Months went by. I was finally ready to drive home to Mississippi. I couldn't stay away from my mother forever. I left for home. I knew that I had chosen the Light. The goodness.

Dutchess and I left in the middle of the night.

I was driving and the radio was static or full of interference or white noise. I figured it was God and the Spirit World. I had to be honest with myself about this new found reality before I went crazy. The world had been created billions of years ago and we as a whole are living only from the history and the knowledge that our ancestors had passed down to us. I began to not a light in the sky. I continued to drive because I simply thought it was some helicopter doing night routings. I did work on the flight deck in the Navy. So, lights in the sky are not unusual.

I drove and drove and Dutchess was sitting in the passenger seat. I listened to the noise and listen to the radio as well. I changed the station and the noise would eventually come back. I figure it was something trying to communicate with me. I still noticed the light following in the sky. It was on the left side of my car.

I rolled down the window to make sure it was not some reflection of some light that was inside of my car. But it was a Light following me. It was clearly not a reflection.

I continued to drive and I'm sure I was somewhere near the Area 51 area. Well, I had watched the television specials of extraterrestrial and paranormal activity. I felt that this was something much different. The Light was more like a star. It could have been aliens but I was on a more spiritual and powerful experience up until now. The boxing match was the most powerful encounter I have had with the Spirit World and the existence of other forces or abilities. I was well aware that I could have pursued love with the guy who took me to the boxing match, but if I was correct, there were now other forces watching me and other abilities that I possessed were coming into maturity.

I drove and drove and eventually out of curiosity, I pulled over at the rest stop to make sure that the Light was following me. There is a saying "whatever is meant for you, is meant for you". This was definitely connected to me and everything and every thought that I had ever had.

I got out of the car at the rest stop and people were there but it was night time. No one was paying me any attention. I let Dutchess out to use the restroom and she ran off into the darkness. I looked up into the sky and saw that the Light was hovering in the sky. Just still.

I lifted my hands and signal at the Light. The Light went black or disappeared and reappeared or turn back on. I signaled again and it signaled back as if it was mimicking or communicating with me. I was amazed and overwhelmed at the same time. Tears came to my eyes but I was not afraid. I knew this was something spiritual or something that I was connected to. I didn't overreact or get anyone's attention to notice the Light. I simply waited for Dutchess to finish using the restroom and when she returned, I got back into the car with her and cried myself to sleep.

I wondered who I was or what was I capable of if I focus on the signs that are definitely in existence. I wondered about the voice that spoke at the boxing match. I thought about the way the Universe had answered my prayers.

The rays of the sun felt different when I woke up the next morning. It's hard to explain. But, I felt more connected to the Universe and space and time. I thought about the beginning of time up until now and all that had been created. It was a feeling of fear and a feeling of comfort that came over me. There were so many voices or thoughts running through my mind. The sun felt as if it was feeding me through its rays. I lay there in the car getting my thoughts together about the Light that was no there when I woke up. Where did it go? What was it? Why did the rays of the sun feel so different?

I turned on the car and there was no sound on the radio. I checked other stations and there was nothing. I thought… "It left". I thought the car repaired but I was far from Mississippi. I drove anyway and eventually sound returned to the car after a few miles. I thought to myself… "Am I in control of any of this? Is it something that is trying to communicate with me or was it something wanting to use me in any way?

I drove and drove and eventually we reached Mississippi. I went to my grandmother's grave and Dutchess and I walked the graveyard and visited all my ancestors.

I have an older brother who died at birth that was buried there. A tree had grown over his grave. For some reason, Dutchess went to the tree and began to scratch the bark off the tree. I was amazed because my brother was only a year older than me and it was a possibility that we could have share the same birth cycle because it was less than a year that he died that I was born.

Regardless, I was amazed and thought…."Could the Light have been brother whom had passed away knowing that I was coming to visit the grave.

I took a video of Dutchess scratching the bark off the tree and immediately call my mother and let her know that I was home in Mississippi. She was so happy. It had been almost two years since she had seen me in person.

I met her at the local store. Well… it's the local store. I didn't really have to meet her… she was already going there for her usual cigarettes and beer. She gave me huge hug. I immediately asked her to come sit with me in the car and she did. She immediately asked me, "What the hell is wrong with your car". I looked at her and to keep it simple, I said, "It's God or something". She said, "What do you mean Shaun?". I explained to here that the noise hadn't gone away and I showed her my hand. The marks had long healed but you could see the blemishes on the knuckles of my peace fingers.

She really couldn't deny much because I was showing her and she always had said, "Showing is better than telling". She left her car parked at the store and took a ride with me up the road. She kept saying, "Shaun, you have powers." Tears were coming to my eyes because I had never heard that before and if so, how could I use them. I knew I wanted to only do good. But most importantly, I wanted to keep my family safe.

We drove for a little while and the noise only intensified. I guess the Universe loved the bond that my mother and I have. I showed her the video of my dog scratching the bark off the tree where my brother Monte was buried. She was amazed. She cried because that was where my brother was buried. She then said, "That's a good dog you have if she did that." I agreed. We both looked at Dutchess who was in the back seat listening to our conversation.

I was only home for the weekend, so we immediately drove to her sister's house. She has 13 sisters. It was going to be many visits. I hadn't been around the entire family in a long time. It was a beautiful feeling. I felt like the ancestors were pleased.

After a while sitting with my family on my mother's side, I wanted some time to myself because I was honestly feeling like I was a third wheel. They were used to be around each other daily and I had been gone for so long. On top of that feeling, I didn't what they knew or realized about what I was experiencing. How and why was I born into this unique family of mostly women? I felt at home regardless.

I went to go and sleep in my car with my dog while everyone stayed in the house and continued talking. A few hours had passed and something awakened me. The Light that had followed me was now even bigger and brighter and going across the night sky. I thought it was a helicopter, but it was too big for a helicopter. I did not know who else in the neighborhood was awake or if they even noticed the Light. The Light just went across the night sky above my Aunt's house.

I didn't bother to awaken anyone because I figured it was

something spiritual and related to what I was already experiencing. I felt like it would be overwhelming and it was too brief for me to even have the chance to show them. I just stayed in the car with Dutchess and fell back to sleep.

The next morning we all left my Aunt's house. I went to the lake to meditate and sit for a while. The white noise was still on my radio and the day was rather cloudy. It had begun to rain and there was a flock of ducks flying above head in a circular formation. They flew around in a circle for the entire time that I was at the lake. On the radio, all I heard about was the California wildfires. California was in a drought. I felt the need to go back to California because I felt connected in some way. It was where I had my most spiritual moment.

We left the lake and I went to my parent's house. I told my mother that I was going to be heading back to California. I was crying and she ask why was I crying. I said I had to get back to take them water. I knew that she would not understand, but a part of me felt that she would. I had only come to see her for her birthday and to visit my grandmother's grave.

I gave my mother a kiss on the forehead and Dutchess and I left for California.

I got in my car and the radio was full of static. I drove for a few hours. The noise was on every station. I simply focused on driving. Dutchess got in the front seat and sat upright. She just continued to look forward. The night sky was filled with stars. I could not find a good station to listen to on the radio so I thought that if I put a cd in the player that would make a difference.

Dutchess kept pressing her paw into my hand as if she was trying to get my attention. All I could think about were the wildfires in California, leaving my mother so quickly, and the ducks fly around above the lake in a circle. For some reason, I felt connected. I continued driving. Playing CDs was much more relaxing than listening to the radio. However, every time the cd would skip I would think it was because of the spiritual or some cosmic interference. I would try to listen to the radio but it was too much white noise.

Eventually I made it outside of Texas after driving about six or seven hours. There was nothing but desert and highway. I notice the stars seemed to get bigger and closer, but I thought nothing of it. The Star or the Light that followed me from California was still on my mind.

The cd players began to skip constantly so I turned the radio back on. There was still a lot of white noise. I chose not to flip through stations and just listen to the white noise. It had been with me since the day I got the mark on my hand and even before that I would notice flickering lights or interference on the televisions but I never thought anything of it all. I continued driving and Dutchess kept pushing her paw into my hand. I figured she either had to use the restroom or she really wanted my attention for something that was about to happen.

I continued driving. The stars seemed to come closer in the night sky, but I still thought nothing of it. I was more interested in the noise and the voices that seemed to come across the radio through the white noise.

Throughout history, there has been many sightings of UFOs, paranormal activity, and spiritual presences all over the world. I had reached Texas and New Mexico area. I was getting ready to pull over at a rest area but for some reason, the white noise on the radio stopped. I could not find a station on the radio anywhere but the talk radio station. The stars or the lights in the sky had definitely moved. I'm sure that Dutchess and I were in a remote area of the desert. While driving at about 80 miles an hours about seven lights surrounded the car and a voice on the radio said "You don't care if they come".

The Light or spiritual entities or lifeforms that were very present around the car retreated back into the darkness of space. In my heart I knew that something was trying to communicate with me. I continued driving to a more populated area. I got off at the exit and a car behind me exited with me. The driver followed my car to the gas station and got out of their car to ask me if I was okay. I said "Yes" and acted as if there was nothing more to discuss. The driver asked me if I say the Lights on the freeway. I said "Yes". I was amazed that she had seen what I had seen but I had already experience a lot since the marks on my hand. I was simply trying to understand what the universe was showing me.

I kept my conversation short with the lady because I did not want to draw attention to the event that had taken place. I knew other saw what I saw because the DJ on the talk radio station was talking as if he wanted others to call into the radio station and talk with him about the spiritual or terrestrial occurrence that had taken place.

I finished pumping my gas and let Dutchess use the restroom. We got back in the car and continued driving as if nothing had taken place. I thought to myself, "Did Dutchess know that this event was about to happen. How many others saw or experienced what I had experienced. Most importantly, I was not about to call anyone without further proof or without having a witness. All I knew was that my reality had been altered in that very moment. I drove from that moment to California and made the adjustment to my reality. I knew that more was to come in this new found knowledge of existence. I just wanted to know… Why me?

Evolution has been a big question throughout time. I definitely believed in a lot about creation and the Creator. The idea of being made in GOD's image and likeness had a different understanding or perception that being a produce of reproduction alone. Of course, we are born from or parents and according to the Bible we came from the dust and carry the essence or the parts of the Spirit of GOD who created the Heavens and the Earth. I was granted enlightenment through many of my lessons and encounters with the Creator/ GOD/ Spirit of the Universe. But I began to question which came first, GOD or the Universe, if the Bible says that the God that we know and understand only created the Heavens and the Earth. To be honest with myself, I had to accept the fact that I had no witnesses that I chose to discuss the events that had happened. I was still trying to understand the connection of the reality. I had been able to speak with some entity which I considered as the spirit of the original God who created the Heavens and the Earth. If not, I had no other explanation. I knew I didn't want to overwhelm anyone with this knew revelation of existence. I was simply grateful that the encounter was peaceful.

I believe in the Bible, but to be completely honest.... I consider the Bible as a history book. I believe in GOD much more that I believe in the Bible. I just wanted to know why was I contacted or connected to the encounter that occurred up until now.

# 19

Dutchess and I arrived back in Los Angeles with nowhere to go. I could have easily lived with my parents at home, but I felt like the Universe had me on a different path. I had clearly been exposed to the new understandings of existence. I did not want to overwhelm my family with the events that were going on in my life at the moment.

I parked near the Hollywood Bowl under the cross. I cried every day for about a month. For some reason, it rained a lot and that helped with the fires. I felt very connected to nature but I thought about what my life meant to the Universe or GOD as a whole. What parts of GOD flowed through my veins. Why was the Spirit World watching over or reaching out to me.

I was still off work on medical leave for my eyes. After the experience I had in the desert, I decided to keep the eyes that I was born with. I figured that if I needed surgery in the future, the help would still be there. I honestly felt like I was evolving in existence. I wanted to understand what was happening to me and if I could communicate or use the gift to help others. The white noise on the radio, the Lights that seemed to come from outer space in the desert, the voice on the radio, the experience at the boxing match, the two watches, and the mark on my hand was enough to make anyone questionable about the paranormal or spiritual and alien existence.

I was experiencing a lot when the events began. I had found a lifeless bird when I was walking with my cousin and his girlfriend. I picked up the bird and my cousin kept saying that the bird was dead. I felt as though I should bury the bird or at least see if I could do anything. I pressed into the birds' chest and gave it a few drops of water. My cousin thought I was wasting my time but after a few minutes of walking and talking the bird began to move. It wasn't long before it wanted to be free of my hands. My cousin and his girlfriend were amazed. That experience made me wonder what more I could do.

Most importantly, in my new relationship with GOD and the Spirit World, I wanted to know what did I truly have control or influence over and how was I going to maintain a good reputation in the eyes of future witnesses. If the ancestors, both mine and others, are actually needed my assistance to communicate between physical and spiritual worlds, how do I know when I was making a difference.

I knew of Shamans, Witch doctors, priest, and other practitioners, but I did know if what I had experienced was going to be taken well. Even more, I didn't want to open the door to any negative, evil, or demonic forces in my effort to interact with the living people and those whom have passed on. The Universe or GOD seemed to know that I had enough free time on my hands to allow the presence of other forces or entities to guide me and allow me to guide others in their healing or search for understanding.

I was already studying in Respiratory Therapy which dealt in the

"Breath" so to speak. So my connection to the Spirit of GOD and the energy or Breath that flows through us. I had met a few people who had loved ones who were on life support or hospice care. I knew that from the moment the marks appeared on my hand that everything thing that had happened to me, regardless of directly or indirectly, was because my thoughts, my prayers and my unfinished intentions all mattered and were a part of a big puzzle or major ingredient to understand the whys and the how's in reference to the journey we all began from the cosmos to conception; to life; to death, and rebirth in our next lives. If I could communicate to the Spirit World or the Spirit World was trying to communicate or remind me of a life I had already live or was meant to live, I wanted to be able to live it without fear or simply with the understanding that fear would always be present in lack of understanding.

I decided to take a job watching over a person who was in a coma. I did not ask for any compensation. Well, I simply said to the person who hired or trusted me, "you only pay me if there is improvement".

The job was in San Francisco near Lincoln Park, somewhere close to Stanford and Berkley University. The client was cop. He and his wife had a son who had been injured in a water skiing accident. He was in a coma and paralyzed from waste down. He had a two sets of twin brothers and another set of five identical brothers. They were very well off but the medical expenses were becoming unbearable with no signs of hope. If I didn't have anything, I had hope. The family was mixed with Jewish and Italian bloodline, amongst other races. The really were very beautiful, and kind. But mostly concerned with losing their loved one forever. I could feel their pain.

I asked for family to tell me everything about him and if it was okay to be comfortable to touch him while I cared for him. The reality of the matter, the family had no clue that I was gay and I didn't know if any of them were possibly gay. Most importantly, I want them to understand that if my methods worked to bring their loved one back from the coma or near death stat of being, then they need to be aware of the necessary nurturing that would be required for the loved one to desire to return from the coma or place of limbo. I said they may wake up desiring me sexually, or even feeling offended or violated by the sight of me or them. I wanted them to know that the loved one may not return as the person they were before the coma because to the growth or deterioration of their spirit with them.

The cop's son was very intelligent, a super athlete, and attractive. Just like all the rest of his brothers. The house was like a castle filled with marble, granite and lime stone. I could feel the love they had for him and the grief they felt in holding on. He had a friend who was a girl, but they had previously been involved and had broken up before the accident. So I asked her if she had any type of loving feelings toward him still or was she just there in support of his recovery. I could see that she was putting two and two together in regards of my mannerisms and possible sexuality. But I was not to simply assume that she or he was completely heterosexual. I simply wanted here to know that while I was treating or caring for him. It would require touch and talk and lots of mental reinforcement from the Spirit World. She seem to understand.

I had very long hair. Dreadlocks down to my ass. I was very toned and muscular and I thought of myself as attractive based on the comments I had been given. Basically I was very androgynous. I appeared as both masculine and feminine. I knew that caring of this level would have moments of intimacy that would not intentionally be sexual but with someone in a coma, I believed they were somewhat aware of the space or place that their comatose body was in, but not in control of how their body reacted to the stimuli around them. Meaning….. he could think that I was her touching him and move in a normal reaction and react to me as if I were here. In that moment I would have to either control him or pretend to be her because the goal was to make him choose "Life".

The cop, or the father who hired me to look after his son had brothers whom were his identical twins as well. In fact, there were seven in his set of brothers, then all seven of them had another set of four twins, then triplets. So to maintain focus I definitely could not remember everyone's names. They just respected the I was trying to accomplish a task to bring him out of the coma.

After getting all the details of how I was to approach the process, I began. I got all his favorite music and the things I knew he loved. His brother Vinni and I became very close. The majority of his family was busy getting their degrees in different fields. Some of them were even beginning schools. They would stop by and visit on occasion but they got used to me being there every day.

I informed the previous girlfriend that I was making a playlist of music and recording everything that was going on. I wanted the family to trust me but I mostly wanted to earn their respect by letting them see me do everything. There were many uncomfortable moments. I remember the time of year was around Mother's Day. By the time Father's Day came around, he was having minor moment in his lower body. It was definitely a sign of improvement.

I was becoming more that a health care provider to he him and I was being seen in a different Light by the family.

Eventually they started to question the "hows" and "whys" of what I was doing. The work was very demanding because it was all faith based. I could see what I was doing and see the outcome before it happened with no guarantee or proof that it would. I was always alone with him, other than the previous girlfriend and the mother. The father was always at work as a detective.

After the improvement in his condition was undeniable, the family was becoming more affectionate towards me and they had a different understanding for me. The father came home one day in the middle of lunch and I was in my relax clothes. His son was still in a coma but he had some reflex or response to touch and smell. The father caught me off guard with a very long hug. He was telling me how grateful he was that I was even trying to help. Especially with no request for payment. He continued to hug me and could feel his body heat and his breath alongside my face as we were face to face in a deep embrace.

He then kissed me on the jaw and looked me in the eyes and I looked over at his son. He then said how beautiful I was and hugged me again for about fifteen seconds and walked out. I didn't want to overthink the kiss on the jaw but I wasn't expecting it and the father was very attractive.

His son was show more and more signs of improving or choosing Life over death. His brother Vinni would come all the way from San Francisco to Hollywood to hang out as friend. But I didn't know that some of the members were becoming attracted to me....

After being questioned about what I had done or what I was doing, some of the people were skeptical or questioning my credibility. For some reason, they wanted me to take a lie detector test. I agreed to it and passed.

The family was getting the signs of improvement that they had lost hope in and I was getting confirmation in the authority or influence I had in healing and restoration. Human nature and natural behavior was about to begin as well as the side effects of operating on a spiritual level. Understanding the balance of Life and

Death. I wanted them to be happy if he lived a little longer and the Universe or GOD chose to call him back to his new beginning. I did want any negative or dark energy or spirit to attach itself to him if he chose life and woke up from his coma. I knew I was neglecting a lot of my own needs in this process and I knew that psychological, spiritually or angelically I was now or somehow capable of at least restoring hope in his family. I knew id have no control over his desires when he woke up and realized it was my voice and presence that he heard while in the coma... talking him back to choosing Life.

Meanwhile, Dutchess was always near. The family was pet lovers and Dutchess had gotten protective and attached to them as well. My relationship with the family and the people they knew had become much more than just professional. I guess you can say I became romantic with overtime and began to see more variety in the way people loved each other. I can say I actually felt love. And I began to let my guard down and embrace to thought of someone actually wanting to love me. But nevertheless, I was maintaining focus on his son because he hadn't completely woke up yet.

California has it set of cultures and races and beliefs. Gay rights were becoming law in many parts of the world and same sex marriage was becoming legal. The wild fires were happening and there was an earthquake in 2006 that caused a tsunami to come across to California. I was at the beach in Huntington Beach and bamboo was brought across the ocean. I thought about the power of nature. It was enough to give a temporary distraction from the mental exhaustion of loving a twin and his brother who was in a coma.

The mother of the cop's son was named Jackie. She already knew that one or more of her sons were gay or bisexual and attracted to me. She and I became friends because she understood my struggle with my sexuality and my attraction to her son and a few of her other family members and how I was try to tap into a part of existence and reality that most are afraid of or overlook. She even knew of her own husband's sexual appetite and she found it sometimes amusing, yet admirable. She comforted me one day by walking in on her son and I laying in bed together. She cooked us breakfast and invited me on a camping trip that they usually went on anyway every summer. Somewhere near Big Bear Mountain.

I agreed to go because I still had not returned to Verizon for work yet. I was still out on medical leave for the Corneal Transplant which had honestly decided not to attempt, not because of the healing process; but because I could feel some sort of energy. I chose to wait until I simply went blind and just use hard contact lenses to correct my vision. I could feel heat or fire in my eyes…. A soothing fire but yet different.

The brother whom I was falling in love with was named Malcolm. Well… in this world there as cases of twin cousins. Malcolm was the son of Jackie who was interested in photography. He volunteered of the fire department and looked like all is other brothers but was not in the set of a twin. He was often with Vinni or simply by himself. Anything I need around the house while taking care of his identical cousin who was in a coma, he would get it for me. He was actually the one of the brothers who proposed to me and because he was the most relaxed, I agreed. But only if he could respect that his older brothers were already interested in me. He agreed. Malcolm was unique to me because it was Jackie as well who had her own identical twin sister who was a professor at Stanford. She was married to the cop's brother. The cop's brother was also in school studying paranormal psychology. They reminded me of the Jetsons family cartoon. They understood that what I was doing had some connection to the unexplainable. They were the reason the cop requested the lie detector test.

One day we were at the beach in San Francisco and I was walking in the ocean on the rocks and stepped on a poisonous fish. Since was already off work but working for the family and in love with one of their members I stayed at the house in the bed sick with my own near death experiences. I could feel the family checking on me and on some days crying as I lay in a deep sleep taking strong antibiotics. The brother of the cop, who was already a doctor was afraid of losing his license if he gave me the wrong medication. They had cameras all throughout parts of their house. He said that it was as if time slowed down and real time went on around us. Miraculously, my fever broke and I woke up and immediately went back to working and taking care of the cop's son. While in my state being I had an out of body experience. There days it was as if my body had flat lined and the cop's brother was crying over me. I felt paralyzed but aware. But my connection to the cop's son was a part of me surviving stepping on the fish at the beach. Dutchess was by my side the entire time. Malcolm was there as well.

The cop's brother was even more amazed. Malcolm was pretty much his nephew. But even his son was attracted to me. They all would hold and kiss me on my forehead as I slept and the swelling went down. It was time to go camping. There was a lot of love around me and it was feeling like I was coming into some sort of control of my gifts or powers. I could hear the voice of GOD and the Spirit World. I was trying to maintain focus.

## 20

knew that I was not crazy. Yes, I was diagnosed with PTSD because of the true story of my life that I told my psychologist at the time. In a session, we only get thirty minutes to an hour to inform the therapist of anything new in your life. I couldn't inform them of the treatment that I was giving the cop's son because it wasn't conventional or traditional medicine. I knew that the moments and the experiences that I was having were not going to understood from just me telling them. So I kept my appointments simple and within the "common reality" of the world as we know it.

I was too deeply connected to everything around me. I had now fallen in love but I felt as though I was not going to be able to enjoy it completely. I understood life comes with challenges. I didn't want anyone that I loved going through anything painful because of their relationship to me. It was enough in life to be hated for my skin color, but to be hated because of my sexuality or how and whom I chose to love or allow to love me was stressful.

Within the family of cops and from Malcom I felt no sign of hatred. The cop's son who was in the coma was showing more and more signs of improvement and movement. He hadn't awakened yet but his body wasn't deteriorating from lack of motion. The entire family had come to respect the space and the house as I worked. I was still healing from the sting of the poisonous fish. But I felt that I somewhat became more connected to nature and the Spirit World. I could hear silent whispers reassuring me that the fact that I cared about the cop's son, was somehow giving him something to hold on to within the world of the living and to Listen to in the void of the Spirit World. He was on in his condition because of the accident from water skiing. I wasn't his time to die. He was in the void of Life and Death.

I believe in multiple Universe. I understood that the Bible states that GOD says "Place no other gods before Me. Once I receive the marks on my hand, I had confirmation of the "other side". The Divine connection between human, spiritual and animal experiences. Sort of like the movie "Golden Compass".

At the boxing match when I was on my date and the birds were hovering over the section I was siting in; the Sun rushing behind the clouds as the conversation I was having with my date brought up Voodoo. There was a guy of Latin or Indian decent sitting next to me as the voice from the Spirit World came over the sound system and spoke words that I had imagined or recalled the Voice saying to me prior to the marks appearing on my hand.

That guy was confused about the Voice and the reason it spoke over the audio or sound system. He yelled at me and asked me "Do you want It to come back" as we were leaving the boxing match. I didn't have to answer but I knew I had a witness of a very short conversation and confirmation from GOD or the Spirit World that I represented a relationship that had long been thought dead. The family, as far as I knew didn't have any idea of that experience with GOD. They were amazed at the recovery of their loved one and that alone was enough to convince them of the possibility that this was my "Calling" or "Life Path".

I felt and believed in all my heart and soul that all life mattered. I felt somehow able to communicate with the Spiritual, Animal and Human world on a different level. It was very tiring and sometimes distracting to others because it caused me to be very quiet because my mind was listening to thoughts or voices of assurances as I cared for the cop's son. I thought about my own personal family and how everyone alive on the planet are Divinely connected. I believed that life existed throughout the Universe. I could see myself or my spirit in other places….. in another body, time, and dimension. I definitely believed in a higher power or a version of GOD that has the final say so over all Life. I believed I was a part of that divine connection in the "crossing from life to death". The static on the radio, the high pitch whistle I would sometimes hear, and just the relationship I had to nature and animals made me feel connected.

Because of my upbringing, I was not someone who care to question people. Mostly, because of respect for their personal lives. Now I was in an environment with people who were talkative and expressed their love and concern for one another. I had become comfortable with the respect they had for me. What I was attempting to do for the cops son was only the beginning of my ability to care for someone. The process was unpredictable and unexplainable because I was not relying on the visible sources. It felt very sacred and spiritual. I knew GOD was present every step of the way. It simple felt good to have witnesses.

I spent a lot of time with Malcolm. I had made plans to be transferred to a store in San Francisco with Verizon when I returned back to work. I was committed to my understanding of what the cop's son was going through in his coma. We had decided that since he was aware that other guys were interested, we'd just let our relationship take its course. I was just trying to focus on the names of all the sets of twins I was meeting. I never felt any form of racism or discrimination.

We finally went on the camping trip. It was just for a weekend. The plan was to allow the cop's son to get some fresh air and get to know Malcolm and his family better. I was well aware of what was going on in my life without the presence of other people. It had been a long time since I tried to do anything normal... so to speak.

We got to the camp site and everyone began unpacking. I went for a walk to get some fresh air and to clear my head. It had been a few months since I had spoken to anyone that I was related to... I was finding a new place in the work that I was now doing. I knew that GOD or the Universe was trying to show me a new life and a new way of living.

## 21

The camping trip only made us closer as well as apart. The cop's son was showing much more signs of improvement. He had actually awakened from his coma. His best friend came running to me and was so happy. The family was overjoyed. I was happy as well. I felt as though my work was done. It was time for me to let go of the work that I had done for the cop's son. His regular doctors had taken over the care of his son. There was nothing that I could do anymore. I didn't get any recognition for the care I provided. It was simply…he woke up and the doctors who already had their reputations took over. I felt no need to fight to continue because they were in professional hands.

Malcolm and I began to no longer be involved because I had no reason to continue coming around his family.

I knew that I was going to always end up alone. I would either loose contact with my friends or they would loose contact with me. I was never one to force any kind of relationship. Now being exposed to the Spirit World and learning day by day, I knew my life might

129

be too overwhelming for someone to actually love me or truly care about me.

Slowly but surely I began to retreat back to the normal things that were going on in my life. The things that had always happened. I knew what I was capable of in my experience with the cop's son. I just did know how to go about doing it on a regular basis. It really is an emotionally draining process to believe that I was assisting someone in choosing life. In addition to that, it was more draining because the people around them grew to love me and appreciate me....but I know that I shouldn't make any personal connections because of the job.

I was in the middle of trying to find out my new purpose or calling in life and trying to know what I had control over. I did not want to leave anyone behind on my journey and I definitely didn't want to give any free rides to anyone who was not trying to make the world a better place. I thought a lot about Jesus. A whole lot.

If Jesus came back or was born again, how would we really know? Was I the new version of Jesus? What would Jesus be able to do? I thought about the possibility that Jesus could have already come back and may have already been killed again.

The family wanted to pay me for what they considered as bringing their son out of the coma. I took the money because I needed it. They insisted that I take the money and said that I had powers. I asked that they keep the knowledge of my powers to themselves because I was still new to my gifts.

They were amazed at the camping site. They had never seen someone interact with the Spirit World like I was.

It was good to have witnesses around, but when they left or I was alone I would need extra confirmation that some things had taken place. I didn't have anyone to talk to. Most of what I had to talk about seemed unreal, which made things even harder.

I was in a new stage of evolution. I didn't know if there were others like me or if I was the only one. My feelings for Malcolm were strong, but not strong enough to get him involve in the life that happening. I put my love for him on hold and focused on a normal life.

It felt like I had to keep it a secret because many people would not understand. It had been a long time since there was spiritual healer or anyone that specialized in the Spirit World. Most importantly, I was not trying to be seen as "evil" in my efforts to help others or explain my actions as I went along in life. There was a lot that I was going to have to give up on the opportunity because of the chance of being misunderstood. Somehow, I was going to have to find balance in between the reality that was once normal and this new reality that seemed so spiritual and magical. The ways of the ancient ones seemed to be resurfacing and I didn't know who to go to in order to communicate or share knowledge or experiences. I had witnesses, but those witnesses were sometimes in amazement. Even I was trying to figure out how much control or power I had in my efforts to heal or enlighten others.

I knew my time with the cop's son and his family had come to an end. The experience with them was the most rewarding on this new journey since my "Stigmata". If it wasn't my doing alone, I knew that something in the Universe was constantly with me. Whether it was GOD or not, I was still trying to decide. Honestly, I heard voices and could even see something that others could not see which was amazing and left me unable to describe. I just knew it was powerful, spiritual and now a part of my everyday life.

I knew that my efforts to bring the cop's son out of his coma had worked. I had to figure out who I was in the world and why the Universe allowed me to help. I still had to live and go on with life while doing so. I noticed every noise, every little event, every encounter I had with new people. It was impossible for me not to question why everything was happening. Ironically…. I found myself completely quiet. Sometimes I would go for days and weeks without saying much to anyone. In my phone calls I found myself just listening and agreeing. It had been a long time since I had been around anyone other than for work.

I thought about Malcolm a lot. For the first time I felt love from a man but the Universe was putting more and more on my plate. I thought about the guy who took me to the boxing match and the voice took over the microphone and spoke over the speakers. I thought about GOD and how HE/SHE possible felt about me.

I thought about the marks on my hand and how Moses was glowing when he came down from the mountain after talking to GOD. I thought about the statement that GOD made, "Place no other gods be for ME". I thought about a life without the thought or presence of GOD. Love filled every thought. Fear brought understanding. I thought about reincarnation and the Afterlife.

I was lucky because I had already worked a lot of good jobs. I was able to relax and not be obligated to go to work at my age. The free time gave me the opportunity to help the cop's son. It put me in a place to receive love in all forms. I can say it was perfect time meeting such an open minded family. The fact that there were a lot of twins gave me a different perspective on personalities of people. They help me to find balance and heal.

Life was pretty slow paced for me. I slowly went back to the wilderness…so to speak. My phone never rang and if it did, it was my mother. All of my friends were living their lives and it had been years since I had spoken to them. There had not been any love lost, it was just that life had take us all down different roads. I was not working and did not return back to Verizon Wireless because I was satisfied with the income I was receiving. I looked at it as a blessing and called it retirement at the age of 30.

I lost track of the cop's son and Malcolm. Not a day goes by that I think of them. I knew that I had to make sure that the things that were happening were real. Some part of me did not want the love that I shared with Malcolm to be based on the fact that I had a part in healing his cousin. I didn't want to pull Malcolm into any danger that may come from the Spirit World because I was still new to my experiences.

Dutchess and I found an apartment in Beverly Hills. I figured it was peaceful and close to the Veterans Affairs Hospital. It was January when we moved in and the apartment was all hardwood floors and on the first floor. I had somewhat kept in touch with my cousin and because of blood relation I forgave him for his past behavior. I allowed him to sleep over a few nights. Besides….he was living with me when he marks appeared on my hand and we were talking about Zoroastrianism.

Every morning I would get up and go on my normal walk through the neighborhood. Some mornings I would give money to the children at the crosswalks on their way to school. I felt it was a form of giving back. It gave me some sense of normalcy.

My cousin was still trying to get on his feet. So I didn't mind him coming and living with me again. It was good to have someone else in the apartment other than Dutchess. I didn't mention the marks on my hand and neither did he. I honestly didn't think he remembered the marks ever being on my hand. I didn't want to overwhelm my cousin with the spiritual events that were going on in my life. I didn't believe he was mature enough to handle what I was going through.

My cousin and I loved each other because we grew up with each other. Now we were grown men and I expected him to keep his word on most of what he said. I guess it was my military background or it was just based on the principles of life in general.

I was somewhat getting used to the apartment. Overtime, I wanted my cousin to take up more responsibility if he was going to continue living with me. Honestly, we had two different perspectives on life. He felt as though I was doing nothing with my life because I wasn't leaving out going to work every day. I felt that all he wanted to do was have sex with many different girls…. Eventually, my cousin came to my apartment in the middle of the night. He was beating on the door. I don't know why I chose to get upset but I did. I guess I really upset my cousin because he cut three of my tires on my car. That brought me back to reality. Nevertheless….I still loved my cousin.

A few months went by and the only communication I has was with my mother. The static was still on the radio. I just considered it as the ancestors or the spirit world trying to communicate with me still. I ignored it by playing CDs and using the internet for music. However, if I had company and person was really experiencing some loss in faith or a spiritual matter, I would allow them to hear the static or "white noise" that was on the radio.

Honestly, the world had a lot going on and I was just one human being trying to figure out my place in the world. I did not want to be a disappointment to GOD and the Spirit World. I didn't want to embarrass my family in any kind of way.

A few more month went by and I was getting more comfortable in the apartment. I had become acquainted with the neighbors on the first floor. They seemed pretty nice. The father would always offer me things that he was trying to let go of from the apartment. Sometimes I would accept them just to be nice and other times I would turn down the offer because I didn't want to owe him anything.

I had a lot of free time. The days were long. I reconnected with Paul. He and I shared and interest in music and began working on a song together. When he first saw me he said "I thought you were dead". It had been almost a yr and a half since we had seen each other. I loved talking and sitting with him. Even though we hadn't seen each other in a while...it seemed like we had not lost any time. Paul was very attractive. He always talked about a metaphysical world. We smoke a lot of weed together. He loved Dutchess and enjoyed our company. Before long, Paul and I became intimate with each other. It was amazing. But, just like every other moment of intimacy, it did not last long.

It was the month of October and life was going as usual. We got some new tenants that moved into the apartment above me. Everything had been going well. For some reason the police were called to the apartment complex. I was in my apartment and didn't know why they wanted to speak to me. I had no warrants and no tickets. I chose not to let the police in and they went away. I didn't think anything of it.

The next day I went outside and began working out. Out of nowhere, the police came. They taped me and slammed me down to the ground. They took me downtown to the jail station in Beverly Hills. I had a busted, bloody chin. They tried to search me and I wiped my blood on the wall of the jail cell. They then decided to transport me downtown and tried to give me some sort of medical attention. I refused the medical treatment and wanted to know why they had brought me there. I said that I would get my medical treatment from the Veterans Affairs Hospital. They began to ask me if I knew why I was there. I said "No". I guess they decided that there was no reason to hold me and they released me. For the first time I felt like I was being watched to a certain extent.

I walked all the way home through Compton and the area of Los Angeles called the Jungle. As soon as I made it to my apartment I began packing. I called my mother and informed her of what the police had done. It only made her worry, so I told her that I was going to move home to Mississippi. Overnight, I call the Beverly Hills Police department and reported what I thought was a form of police brutality. They came and took pictures of my chin. I had already promised my mother that I would come home for a while. The captain of the Beverly Hills Police Department came with them. He said that he didn't want anything more to happen. I said "What more do you all plan on doing to me?" I probably should have pursued legal assistance but I informed the Captain that I was going to be moving back home because of the experience.

I was mostly too embarrassed than I was afraid to continue living in the apartment. I did not want to have my mother worry that the incident would happen again so I was packed up all within one day. I had hired a moving company that didn't want to accept my form of payment so I left all my belongings in the apartment and only took what would fit in my car. I was just upset with the entire experience.

I didn't let the apartment manager know that I was moving out so I lost my deposit. Some part of me felt like I was overreacting, but the other part of me felt like I was being watched and the police had really gotten too close.

I knew I wasn't ready to move back home and I could have just continued to live in the apartment in Beverly Hills, but I got on the road anyway.

I drove home and of course...all the way there, there was static or "white noise" on the radio. When I got home I knew I had outgrown the small town that I still called home. My mother gave me a big hug and asked if I was alright. I said "of course". I had only come home so that she wouldn't worry about the police in California.

It was too crowded to live with my parents so I found an apartment in downtown Memphis, TN. It was about a thirty minute drive from my parents' house. I moved into the apartment on January 15th 2009. It had only been four months since the police incident in California. I had taken up Respiratory Therapy at Concorde Career College in Memphis, TN. I was still a bit upset with the police in California, but I was putting it behind me.

One day I was sitting in the business office of the apartment complex working on the computer and this girl walked in and kissed me on the jaw. I asked her why did she do that and she gave no answer. She just walked out. I only assumed that since I was in hospital scrubs she thought I was a doctor or a nurse and saw me as a source of income. I soon got over the encounter with the girl.

Later I invited one of my younger cousins over to spend some time with me and see some parts of downtown Memphis. We had a great time but I ended up loosing my garage access. After taking my cousin home I came back to my apartment and met the girl who kissed me on the jaw at the door. I asked to use her garage access so I could go to my car.

She called the police and told them that I had stolen her keys. When I returned to the apartment complex the lobby was filled with police. I was walking Dutchess so they maced me and Dutchess as well. I was taken to the Memphis Mental Health Facility for psychiatric treatment...even though I felt as though I had no need for it. The girl had lied to the police and nearly got me killed. I was forced to quit school because I was in the hospital for almost two weeks based on what the girl had said.

Once I got out of the hospital I lost my apartment because of the commotion dealing with the police coming on the property. I wasn't devastated. I just saw it as a part of life. Within four months, I was already being mistreated by law enforcement again. I decided to move back home since I was having too many incidents.

My grandfather and my parents were happy to have me back at home. Everyone had gotten older. The events that happened during my childhood were no longer happening. I enrolled in the local college and majored in biology and chemistry to keep myself occupied. I made new friends on campus. I knew I didn't want to live under my parents' roof for too long because of the need for privacy and independence. I moved into my uncles abandoned house next door to my parents. I felt that it was close enough. They were surprised that I chose to move back home and so was I.

I knew that I needed the time to regain peace of mind. Once again, I could have pursued legal action. However, I didn't want to cause a major scene if the case had to go to trial. I simply took it as a valuable learning lesson. I was definitely human.

For the first moment in time I accepted the realization that I had no control over the "free will" of another human being. I had no one that I could depend on in my immediate corner...other than GOD. My understanding of GOD was changing and growing more and more. Whatever was going to happen was not always meant to be. Sometimes it happens because the options are limited. The options are often limited by choice, not by force.

Printed in the United States
by Baker & Taylor Publisher Services